Back
To the Cross

Back To the Cross

WATCHMAN NEE
Translated from the Chinese

Christian Fellowship Publishers, Inc.
New York

ISBN 0-935008-70-5

Available from the Publishers at:

11515 Allecingie Parkway
Richmond, Virginia 23235

TRANSLATOR'S PREFACE

We today are at the terminal period of the dispensation of grace. The hand of the clock is pointing at the midnight hour. Now is the darkest of the night. Soon, following the gloomiest hour, the day shall dawn. Meanwhile, the Church rushes swiftly towards apostasy, moving farther away from God: the power of darkness is unleashed; its evil influence is as damaging in the Church as in the world. The cross of Christ is the sole light that enlightens the current darkness. It is therefore time for the Church to go back to the cross, to the firm foundation of God. There, sins are cleansed and self is delivered. There, the redemptive facts of God are revealed for us to believe and enter in. There, the power of resurrection is experientially known so that the Church may once again be the true witness of Christ on earth. It is time for God's children to seek for higher life and service, time to review the past and rededicate themselves for the days ahead.

At the closing of this age, the activities of Satan are intensified. How greatly are the children of God being attacked, oppressed and especially deceived. Now is the time for the saints to rise up and exercise the victory of the cross to resist and counterattack the Enemy. How fierce is the battle. Can the saints overcome without being fully armed? Saints of God, arise, stand on the victory of Calvary, and proclaim the victory of Christ. Your King is coming, and the days of the Enemy are numbered.

This present volume is a compilation of various writings and addresses given by Watchman Nee in the early days of his ministry. The passage of time, however, only increases the urgency of these messages which are as relevant today, perhaps even more so, than at the time of their first delivery. Would that God's children might return to the cross and be true followers of Christ crucified. May the Church of God be re-awakened to her calling as the light in the world, holding forth the word of life. May she stand in the victory of Christ and bring back the King of kings and the Lord of lords.

CONTENTS

1 | Died with the Lord*

A. Dead to Sin

When the Lord Jesus was crucified, He not only died in the place of sinners so as to open for them a living way to God and give them eternal life, He took sinners with Him to the cross as well. If the effect of the cross were limited to the substitutional side — that is to say, were limited to that which causes sinners not to perish but have eternal life, the salvation of God would be incomplete. For the one who has believed in Jesus Christ and been saved (see Acts 16.31) still lives in a world where temptations are many and the Devil is actively deceiving people. Furthermore, the sinful nature within the believer frequently bestirs itself so that in spite of his being saved he finds he is not able to overcome sin and be free from it in this present world.

---

*This article, written by the author, was published in *Spiritual Light* magazine in 1924.—*Translator*

For this reason, in saving men, the Savior must accomplish a two-fold work: save people from the penalty of sins, and, more so, save them from the power of sin. By dying on the cross for sinners, He saves them from the penalty of sins, which is the eternal fire of hell. By taking sinners with Him to the cross, He delivers them from the power of sin—that is, from the old nature.

Sin does not come from outside; it is there within us. If sin came from outside, it would have no power over us. But sin dwells within us; hence, it is fatal to us. Temptation comes from outside, and sin dwells within us. Being the descendants of Adam, we all have inherited his nature. This natural disposition is old, corrupted and defiled. Sinful man has this sin factor in him. So, whenever outside temptation comes, it is responded to from within, and thus a sin is committed. For example, due to the presence of a proud nature in us (sometimes this is quite hidden), we are given the opportunity to be proud as soon as outside temptation comes. Because of the heart of jealousy in us, we become jealous when we are tempted to see others' superiority over us. Owing to the fact that we have an anxious nature in us, we become anxious when tempted. Hence, all the sins which people commit come from the old man within.

This old man—the sin factor—is corrupted beyond repair or transformation. It cannot be remade or redeemed. God's way of dealing with the old man is to put it to death. He will give us a new life, a new nature. The old man must die. As to all our sinful acts, the word of God commands us to go to the precious blood of the Lord Jesus and be washed: "the blood of

Jesus his Son cleanseth us from all sin" (1 John 1.7); "unto him that loveth us, and loosed us from our sins by his blood" (Rev. 1.5). All these sins refer to sinful acts which we commit outwardly. But as to the sin factor—the old man—the Scriptures never command us to have it washed. God's word does not say that the old man needs to be washed; no, it says the blood of Jesus Christ washes sins, not washes the old man. The latter is to be crucified. This is the word of God.

Whatever God has done in this world is done in the Lord Jesus Christ. To punish sinners, he has punished the Lord Jesus, for the Latter stood in the place of sinners. To put to death the old man, God caused the Lord Jesus to die on the cross, taking all the sinners along with Him to death. From substitutionary death to co-death—such is the plain statement of the Bible: "One [Jesus Christ] died for all, therefore all died" (2 Cor. 5.14).

This point should be carefully considered lest it slip away from us. A believer (one who has confessed his sins and has been saved by faith in the Lord Jesus) ought to have well in mind that the crucifying of his old man is not an independent act outside of the Lord Jesus; rather, it is accomplished through union with the Lord Jesus. As Christ died, our old man died with Him, too, for it died in His death. The ignorance of this fact explains the failure of many. Believers tend to use their *own* power to crucify the old man. Yet however much they may try, that old man is still alive, because it is absolutely impossible for them individually to crucify the old man outside of Christ. Most believers do this through ignorance. They do not know that apart from dying with Christ, there is no other way to put the old man to death. The old man is to be crucified with Christ.

It is not that we died ourselves but that we died with Christ, even as the Scriptures assert again and again: we "were baptized into his death" (Rom. 6.3); "we have become united with him in the likeness of his death" (v.5); "we died with Christ" (v.8); and in Romans 6.6, we are told, "knowing this, that our old man was crucified with him, that the body of sin might be done away, that so we should no longer be in bondage to sin." We cannot crucify ourselves, nor will we die as a consequence. This "crucified with him" is an accomplished fact which was done at the time Christ was crucified. His death is a fact; His substitutionary death is a fact; and so is our being crucified with Him likewise a fact. This "was crucified with him" in the original Greek grammatical tense carries the thought of "was crucified with him *once for all*." So that this matter of our old man being crucified with Christ constitutes an act which is eternally done at the death of the Lord Jesus on the cross.

Now, what is the outcome of this co-death with Christ? What is the design behind it? What is the consequence of having this sin factor—the old man—crucified? To where does this lead us?

Well, the consequence is, that "the body of sin might be done away." This phrase "the body of sin" is the same as "the old man" mentioned above. It is called "the body of sin" because the sin factor within us is personified, organized and activated. "Done away" means a putting to death, a being rendered powerless. Since our old man was crucified with Christ, our body of sin was put to death, thus rendering it powerless. Believers have all experienced the activations of the body of sin, and they find themselves bound. But if they have faith in the co-crucifixion of the old man, they shall experience the ineffectiveness and inactivity of the body of sin.

Now as to the design behind our co-death with Christ, the Scriptures again provide the answer: "that so we should no longer be in bondage to sin." Before a believer ever realized his co-death with the Lord, he was a servant of sin (Rom. 6.17). Sin was his master, which means the sin factor controlled and directed him. He could not follow his own will, but was forced to follow sin, for sin had authority as well as power over him, just as an earthly master has over his slave. The purpose of having our old man crucified with the Lord is to set us free from sin—that is, from the control of sin. Believers naturally were unwilling to be servants of sin, but due to the lack of the experience of the being "done away" of the body of sin, they had to do what they loved not to do. However, if we have the experience of having the body of sin "done away," we spontaneously arrive at the liberty of the sons of God.

Hence, we have before us three things: a fact—"our old man was crucified with him"; a consequence—"that the body of sin might be done away"; and a design—"that so we should no longer be in bondage to sin."

These three elements are joined together and are not to be separated. Yet now that we know there are fact, consequence and design, how can we enter into them? Is there any condition we must fulfill before we can experience this co-death with Christ? The answer is to believe, for there is no other way.

The way you obtain the substitutionary death of the Lord Jesus is the way to enter into co-death with Him. By faith and not by work, you receive the consequence of His substitutionary death—which is to say, you are free from eternal punishment. And likewise, by faith you may gain the consequence of co-death with Christ —which is to say, deliverance from the sin factor. That Christ died for you is a fact; so is your death with Christ a fact. If you were never to believe in Christ's dying for you, you would never receive the salvation flowing from substitution in it saving you from punishment. And in like manner also, if you were never to believe in the fact of your dying with Christ, you would never have the salvation flowing from co-death in it delivering you from sin. All who believe in the substitutionary death of Christ are saved; and all who believe in their co-death with Christ do overcome. Hence, in order to receive the benefit of Christ's death, be it substitutionary or representative, we have to believe. To believe is what God requires of us. First, believe in Christ's substitutionary death, and then, believe in co-death with Christ.

"Even so reckon ye also yourselves to be dead unto sin, but alive unto God in Christ Jesus" (Rom. 6.11). This word "reckon" is of utmost importance. We all want to "touch" and see if our old man is dead. We always like to "feel" whether our old man is dead or not. Yet, if it depends on our "touch" or "feel," our old man will never die, since he does not die simply because we "touch or "feel." As a matter of fact, the more we "touch," the livelier will be our old man; the more we "feel," the more present will be our old man. The old man is not crucified by "touch" or "feel"; he is crucified through "reckoning."

What is it to "reckon"? To "reckon" is to exercise faith, to "reckon" is to exercise the judgment as well as the execution of the will. "Reckoning" is totally different from "touching" or "feeling." For these latter are related to the senses; but "reckoning" is in the realm of faith and will. Hence, the way to deal with the old man does not lie in the realm of feeling. To say "I do not feel my old man is dead" is totally wrong. The death of the old man does not depend on whether or not you feel it so; it is determined by whether or not you reckon it so.

How do you "reckon"? To reckon yourself as dead to sin is to account yourself as already crucified, that is, to account your old man as already crucified. It is reckoning the cross of the Lord Jesus Christ to be also the cross of your old man. Thus you consider the death of the Lord Jesus to be likewise the death of your old man. Indeed, you deem the time when the Lord Jesus died nineteen hundred years ago as having been as well the exact time of the death of your old man. For the old man having been crucified with Christ is a fact, an *accomplished* fact. In the eyes of God, the sin factor is already dead; and so, we must reckon ourselves to be dead to this sin factor. In our believing from the heart that God will realize in us what we reckon, and in our deciding with the will that we have died to sin, we shall no longer be bondservants of sin.

This "reckoning" is an attitude as well as an action. An action is taken once, but an attitude is constantly maintained. An action is taken as a timely move against a certain matter; an attitude is maintained as a lasting estimation of that matter. We ought to reckon ourselves as dead to sin. This is to say that we should take a singular action of reckoning ourselves as dead, and then follow through by a permanent attitude of reckoning ourselves as indeed dead to sin. Action commences; attitude continues. We ought once and singularly to reckon before God, believing ourselves to be dead from that day onward. Having taking that action, we then need to affirm it daily with a corresponding attitude—that is to say, with maintaining the belief of our being dead to sin.

The failure of many lies here: they have reckoned themselves as dead to sin and have received the truth of their co-death on the cross, but they regard this as a once and forever act. A physical death is a once and forever act, so they imagine the same for the death of the old man—not realizing that it does not work the same way in spiritual matters. They should daily and hourly reckon themselves as having died with Christ. Whenever a believer fails to reckon, his old man is revived. This is why so many find their old man resurrected. Had this been a once and forever matter, we would have no need to be watchful. But we know we *must* be watchful. Just as watching is a constant posture, so the reckoning of the death of our old man needs also to be constant. By knowing this, the children of God will be delivered from many defeats. Such an attitude is not sustained by the thought of the mind, rather is it maintained by the permanent assessment of the will. Consciously or unconsciously, "I count myself as dead."

Here again, though, God's children encounter difficulty. They are troubled by their "forgetting" to reckon. But they have used the wrong faculty. For, reckoning is the judgment of the will, not the consideration of the mind. Whether you overcome or not depends on your attitude of reckoning yourself as dead, not on your memory of reckoning. Through the power of the Holy Spirit and the exercise of your will in maintaining this death attitude, you may consciously or unconsciously possess this attitude, which remains the same whether remembering or forgetting. Naturally, the mind has its place, but it is not necessary for it to affect the will. The will should instead control the mind and cause the latter to help the former in sustaining this attitude.

Let us stand, therefore, on the ground of the cross and let us — daily, hourly, consciously and unconsciously — reckon our old man as dead. This is the secret of overcoming sin and the Devil. We know that sin and the Devil are closely related. If sin does not reign in us, the Devil will have no ground in us.

If believers will understand and accept this aspect of the truth of the cross, apostasy and defeat shall be greatly diminished. Lasting victory is inseparable from constant standing on the ground of the cross.

Nevertheless, even after we take the action and maintain the attitude of reckoning our old man to be dead, the sinful nature in us does not henceforth become annihilated and disappear. For as long as we live in this mortal body, the sinful nature will co-exist with us. To say that our sinful nature can be annihilated in this life is a great heresy. We can deliver the old man to death by the power of the cross of Calvary and render it powerless and withered as though dead, but we cannot annihilate it. Whenever we are careless and unwatchful, whenever we do not stand on the death ground of Calvary, our old man will renew its activities and resume its office. Satan is always looking for an opportunity to reactivate the old man. And as soon as there is a loophole, the old man will recover its original position.

In view of this, we ought to be watchful lest the old man be revived. Is not this most difficult? Indeed, it is hard to the flesh. For this reason, a believer must have the power of the Holy Spirit in letting the cross work in him. The cross and the Holy Spirit are inseparable. On the one hand, the cross makes victory over sin possible to the believer; on the other hand, the Holy Spirit substantiates the accomplished fact of the cross in the life of the believer. A Christian who wishes to be delivered from the power of sin must not make provision for the flesh. He must be watchful and count no cost. He must be more disappointed in himself and place more reliance on the Holy Spirit. To man this is impossible, but to God all things are possible.

The death of the cross is different from other deaths. It is a most painful and a most prolonged kind of death. If we should really reckon ourselves as dead and take the cross of the Lord as our cross, we will suffer great pain and agony in the flesh, for did not the Lord Jesus himself hang on the cross for six long hours before he expired? Unquestionably, then, this death of which we speak is slow and prolonged. So far as the experience of co-death in the Christian life is concerned, it is mainly included in this representative period of six hours. When the Lord Jesus was on the cross, He had authority to come down if He so wished. By the same token, those who are crucified with the Lord can let their old man come down from the cross if they so will. For the old man is crucified through your reckoning by faith. If you firmly maintain that death attitude, your old man will be rendered powerless, as though dead. But if you loosen up, it will become active again.

Many children of God often wonder why their old man is resurrected. They have failed to see that the death of the cross is a prolonged one. The Devil is most alert in finding an opportunity to revive the old man and to cause the believer to sin. Hence, at the time of the believer's negligence, the Devil's temptation and deception will manifest itself. And as soon as the outside temptation and deception arrive, the old man within will respond. It is therefore important to return to the ground of the cross at that moment, and as you resume reckoning yourself to be dead, the Holy Spirit will apply the power of the cross towards you so that the temptation immediately loses its attraction.

Every believer should have this kind of supernatural experience—which is to say, that at the point of defeat, you quickly come to the cross afresh, reckon yourself as dead, and thus receive an influx of the power to resist temptation and keep you from it. Nonetheless, sometimes you may reckon and reckon, but you get no result. Is this because you have sinned? Many believers share this kind of experience. The fault lies in your reckoning. For if you truly reckon, there will be that supernatural power coming to you. Please understand that this "reckoning" is not a reciting with your lips, "I am dead, I am dead"; nor is it a thinking in your mind, "I am dead, I am dead." It lies in the judgment of your will that you *are* dead, supported by your attitude of faith. Your will chooses to say, "I am dead." In other words, you first are *willing* to die, and then you reckon yourself as being dead indeed.

We therefore need to learn how to reckon with will and faith. If we truly stand on Romans 6.11, we will always experience victory. Yet as soon as a believer begins to adopt this attitude, Satan will especially stir up storms and waves to confuse him. During such a time, the believer should quietly depend on the power of the cross made available by the Holy Spirit. He should neither strive nor worry as though the temptation is too great and the Enemy too strong. No, he should simply reckon himself as dead to sin, because the cross has the power to overcome the power of sin.

In the event of defeat, however, you should rise up again and rely even more upon the power of the cross. The Holy Spirit will surely lead you in triumph in the Lord Jesus. Wrote Paul, "Sin shall not have dominion over you: for ye are not under law, but under grace" (Rom. 6.14).

B. Dead to Self

To die to self is, in experience, deeper and more advanced than to die to sin. The children of God usually pay much attention to overcoming sin. They have suffered much in sin. They know how their regenerated life grieves over sinning. They have tasted the bitterness and sinfulness of sin. Naturally, at times like this, their greatest desire and interest is indeed to overcome sin in order that they will no longer be in bondage to it. So that after they receive the light of their co-death with Christ, they will reckon themselves as dead by the power of the Holy Spirit, thus allowing the Spirit to manifest the accomplished work of the cross upon their lives.

Yet just here lies a great danger; they may be inclined to consider this overcoming experience to be the highest life, as though there is nothing more to be added. Because they pay such a great amount of attention to their sin, they feel contented once sin is overcome. Now we should in fact pay attention to our sins. Believers should not be careless about them. Overcoming sin is the foundation of all righteousness, and it is the turning point of the Christian life. We certainly cannot expect to make any progress in spiritual life if sin still reigns over us. But this does not mean that after overcoming sin we can circumscribe its boundary and thereafter stay put. We ought to understand that this is but the *first* step in the renewal of redeemed sinners. The future is quite boundless. Let us not conclude that there is no more advancement. For after overcoming sin, the believer is faced with yet another problem: how to overcome "self."

Believers often misinterpret the real meaning of "self." Some combine "self" and "sin" together into one. They think "self" is the sin factor which must die. Of course, self and sin are unquestionably associated in many ways; nonetheless, self is not sin. Believers use self-measurement to measure all their outward actions. Whatever they deem to be wrong, they condemn it as sin. Such self, being in their minds the sin factor, ought, they believe, to be crucified. They do not realize, however, that though self is evil, it is not *altogether* evil. What issues from the sin factor is doubtless all sinful, corrupted and defiled. When the sin factor manifests itself through self, naturally there is no good. Even so, what sometimes issues from self is, according to human eyes, fairly good, decent, moral and righteous. If we use our measurement of sin to measure self, we will no doubt get rid of the evil part and retain what to men's eyes is the good part. This is because believers do not know the *root* of self—that it can issue forth in what men consider to be good as well as in what men consider to be evil. And thus they will dwell within the realm of "self" and fail to enjoy the full and abundant life of God. How subtle is Satan who always tries to hide this fact from believers and keep them in darkness, causing them to be contented with their sin-overcoming experience but not to seek as well the higher experience of overcoming self.

Self life is the natural life. Influenced by Adam's fall, our natural life is corrupted beyond comprehension. Mankind inherits a sinful nature as the result of the fall of Adam. This sinful nature is closely knitted together with our natural life, which is the self. This self of ours is our "I" which forms our individual personality. In other words, this is our soul. Since the sinful nature is so intimately bound up with self, it is quite difficult to differentiate the latter from the former in their combined action of sinning. For as soon as the sin factor is stirred, self immediately approves and executes. And thus an outward sin is committed.

We cannot distinguish too clearly between sin and self. To an unbeliever, these two appear to be so united that it is hard to separate them. Originally, self took the initiative to sin; but due to its exceeding great power, sin now influences self, even controlling and suppressing it. It induces self to will to sin. Since self is totally depraved through the fall of Adam, it is in complete agreement with sin. Although at times the conscience may raise its feeble protest, such remonstrance is transient and soon disappears. In the life of the unregenerated person, sin and self cooperate perfectly and are fully mingled. For the unregenerated, sin is "self becoming flesh." For them, self is the sum total of the sins of the fallen man. It is not only the source of sin, it is also the phenomena of sin—its root, stems and leaves. Self is simply the original life of sin. The sin of the unregenerated is their self. In short, to them, self is sin.

After a person is born again, and in the initial stage of his Christian life, the believer still maintains this posture of not dividing "sin" and "self." But as he receives more grace from God and as the work of the cross and the power of the Holy Spirit become more evident in his life, he is gradually able to distinguish between these two. During the middle stage of the Christian life the child of God becomes capable of discerning what is sin and what is self. He who has experienced Romans 6.11 often finds victory over sin but not victory over self. From the viewpoint of an advanced Christian, it is much easier to overcome sin than to overcome self. But when a believer possesses the experience of overcoming self completely, he has apostolic life—that is to say, the matured life which the apostles had.

Self life is the life of the soul. Self is our personality and all that it is composed of. From self proceeds our personal idea, flavor, thought, desire, inclination, like and dislike. Self life is the animating power of the person. Let us recognize that the self is *our very self,* including its love and hate. Its life is our *natural* power for doing good. Self is a life which is resident in the lives of those believers who have *not* died to it and is a life which frequently tries to relive itself in the lives of those believers who *have* died to it. In short, self life is a self-centered life.

After a believer has accepted the sin aspect of the work of the cross, the sin factor—which is to say, the sin nature—is paralyzed as though dead, it thus having been rendered inactive. Yet the self life remains *very* active because it has not heretofore been noticed or not noticed very much. During that period of time, this self life is *like* the life of Adam *before the fall.* It is not spiritual, however, since it has not been transformed by the tree of life; nor is it carnal, for it has not yet sinned. In other words, the self of the believer is capable of committing sin or of being spiritual as it wishes. That is why the life of the believer during that period is analogous to Adam's before the fall. It is not spiritual, because it has not been liberated nor has it received the higher life of God. But, then, it is not carnal either, because it has already accepted the finished work of the cross and has reckoned itself to be dead to sin. It therefore belongs to the *self*—soulical, natural and untransformed. Through carelessness, it could fall downward and be defiled by the sins of the flesh. But by advancing into the deeper work of the cross it could become fully spiritual. If it remains in the self-centered realm, it will most likely fall and become carnal.

This, then, is a dangerous stage in the Christian's life. On the one hand, he should watch lest he fall; on the other hand, he should prepare for practical righteousness. The danger is to do good in his own power. This may not be noticeable; often, in fact, it is rather hidden. Sometimes it takes God many years to convince the believer how he is self-possessed and does God's will in his own strength!

What the self includes is very broad. Our will, excitement, affection, intelligence—all belong to its realm. The self is the "I" in each one of us. Its life is the power of my living. The self is the soul, which is a significant element or organ in man. Self life is that life of the soul which is the motivating force of that organ. When a person is in the self stage, his self life imparts its power to the will, excitement, affection and intelligence to do good. Its will has the strength to resist temptations from outside; its excitement creates a sense of joy and of the nearness of God's presence; its affection turns on a deep intimacy with the Lord; and its intelligence causes him to conceive many wonderful teachings of the Bible as well as many methods by which to serve God. Yet these all are done by self and not by the spiritual life of God. Indeed, during this period, God frequently grants special grace to the believer. He gives him many wonderful gifts in order to draw him away from self and to follow the Lord. Yet according to experience, what the believer does and what God has planned are totally opposite. The believer will use these gifts for his own purpose instead of wholly turning to God. These gifts become the "lifesaver" of "self." What untold years and works God must spend on him before he denies self and turns wholly to the Lord!

When a believer receives a deeper knowledge of the wretchedness of self, he is then willing to deliver it to death. What is the way to the death of self? It is none other than the cross. Let us read and consider two passages in the Scriptures which reveal the relationship between the cross and self. The first is: "I have been crucified with Christ" (Gal. 2.20).

What Galatians 2:20 asserts as having happened is something which has been done once and for ever. The moment we realize that self must die, we should singularly exercise faith to confess, "I have already been crucified with Christ." "I" in the original Greek is "ego"—the "I." Aside from the cross, there is no true way of putting the "ego" of self to death. The phrase "with Christ" is also something to be especially noticed here. For the crucifying of self is not an independent act of the believer. He does not crucify himself alone by his own power. Self is crucified with Christ, in union with Christ and together with Christ. This does not imply that I help Christ in crucifying self, because Christ has *already* done it for me—I now simply recognize and believe it to be true.

Furthermore, Christ is the main player here. The passage reads that "I have been crucified with Christ" instead of it saying "Christ has been crucified with me." It is not because, I wishing to die, therefore Christ comes to accompany me. No, no. It is when Christ died that He brought all of my "ego" to the cross to there be crucified. For this reason, I am not *going to be* crucified; rather, I only confess this already accomplished fact. The words "have been" show that this is in truth a fact, not a theory. Our being dead to self is not only possible but is attainable, even factual. The apostles of old had experienced this life of self-death. But so we too may have this kind of life.

This is a *co*-crucifixion, not a *single* crucifixion. Apart from the Lord, we can do nothing. To crucify self with our own power is a myth. It can never be done. Unless we have died in the Lord's death, we will never die. Christ alone in His death brought the old creation and all to the cross. It is foolish and futile to set up another way other than Christ or attempt another plan other than His. Hence, there is nothing left for us to do but to confess that what Christ has accomplished is ours and to ask the Holy Spirit to apply the work of the cross in us.

Simply come to God, deny self and surrender all. Let us deliver our self life, with all that it contains, to the death of Christ's cross by the Spirit of the Lord. We ought to say to God: "Hereafter it is no longer I, no longer my delight, idea, interest and prejudice. I deliver all to the cross. From now on, I will live only for Your will. Lord, it is You, not I." We should thus yield to the Lord and deliver our all to death. This, though, does not mean that henceforth our "self" is annihilated. No, self cannot be annihilated, nor should it be annihilated. Self will remain forever. But if that be so, then, why must self be crucified?

Here we need to understand an essential point: the problem before us is one concerning spiritual *life*. Such a problem lays stress on spiritual experience rather than on literary consistency. Many things might appear contradictory—even beyond reconciliation—in letter; yet, in spiritual life they are quite complementary void of any conflict. The very case before us falls into this category. According to letter, self seems to have died. How, then, is it not annihilated? Do realize that the word "dead" employed here is descriptive of a kind of experimental process. To say the death of self within this context of spiritual life does not suggest that hereafter there is no more self. It says instead that henceforth self will obey God, self will no longer be allowed to sit on the throne—it will be crucified, and all its selfish actions will cease. The self life will no longer be permitted to utilize self. For the self life and its living is now dead. There remains no more self life and its living. What is left is merely its skeleton.

We know the "self" has within it the faculties of volition, emotion and intellect. To believe that our "self" was crucified with Christ does not imply that all these faculties are cancelled out or annihilated. The soulical faculties of a person are never destroyed! To die with Christ simply denotes that self is no longer allowed to rule over its will, thought and feeling but that the Spirit of the Lord is to exercise control over all these faculties of the soul and cause them to obey the life of God within. Unless the self dies, it will never obey the Holy Spirit. The moment our self comes down from the cross, the self returns to its old position. A believer himself has neither the power nor the method to control his self.

But Galatians 2.20 gives us light on this point: "I [the self] have been crucified with Christ ... and ... I now live in the flesh." Paul clearly states in the first clause that he has been crucified with Christ; nevertheless, in the latter clause, does he not also say that his self yet lives? Hence, the crucifying of self does not indicate the *annihilation* of the self; it simply denotes the *cessation of the activity* of the self and the allowing of the Lord to be Lord.

What we have just now discussed is something that is done once and forever. Yet is it sufficient for us merely to believe that our self was crucified with Christ? Is it in truth a once-and-for-all matter? These questions provide an introduction for us to consider the second passage of Scripture we wish to look at closely: "If any man would come after me, let him deny himself, and take up his cross daily, and follow me" (Luke 9.23).

This verse shows us three things we should do; yet actually, they are not three separate things but a single three-fold matter. The *first* step is to *deny self*. To deny means to forsake, to not care, to not be concerned about, to not acknowledge any demand. Denying self means a not letting self rule. This step is a singular action which needs to be taken by specifically believing that "I have been crucified with Christ." In order to protect this step, we must taken another and *second* step, and that is: "take up his cross *daily*." This shows that once we have willed to deliver self to the cross and not let it rule, we then must daily deny self. So that to "deny self" is a "daily" matter—never to be interrupted. To "deny self" cannot only be a once-and-for-all action. Paul declares, "I die daily" (1 Cor. 15.31).

The Lord will give us a cross that we might bear it daily, because self is intensely alert; and Satan, who utilizes self, is untiring. Self is seeking for a chance to be re-enthroned. It will not lightly pass over any conceivable opportunity. Consequently, our taking up the cross daily is most essential.

Here lies the watchfulness required of believers. We ought to daily, nay, hourly, take up the cross that the Lord has given to us. Confess incessantly that the cross of Christ is our cross. Make no provision for self, nor let it have any position. And finally, the *third* step is to "follow me [the Lord]," which is to positively let the Lord be Lord, *fully* obeying the will of God and giving no opportunity nor possibility for self to renew its effort. All three of these steps or stages are centered upon the cross of Christ—which is to say that all three have it as their source. The first step—to deny self—is negative; the second step—to take up the cross—is negatively positive; and the third step—to follow the Lord—is totally positive.

It needs to be added here, however, that these two Scripture passages just now considered should never be separated. Through the combined viewing and practicing of them, we shall always experience the victory over self. At all times we must let the Holy Spirit do His work of implementing in us what the cross has accomplished.

Usually, we will most willingly deliver our bad, defiled, sinful and satanic part of self to Christ and let it be crucified. We are most anxious, in fact, to be rid of this *bad* part of self. Yet we have one flaw: we think we must retain the *good* part of self. In the eyes of God, however, our "self" is corrupted beyond repair because it is fatally and totally flawed by Adam's fall. According to God, except having it crucified with Christ, there is no other way. He will neither heal nor amend our self life. We human beings may be willing to sacrifice our money and time for the Lord, but for us to deny self and have it crucified—*that* we are most reluctant to do. For we conclude that our "self" is not *all* bad. This is according to human observation and is quite natural.

One may not *intentionally* retain his good self. He may keep back the *good* of self *un*consciously, and *consciously* and most willingly deliver the *bad* to death. Yet who knows that if self is not *totally dead*, it is *totally alive?* If the *good* of self is nonetheless living, the *bad* of self is not guaranteed to be dead either. Hence the believer has a serious lesson to learn here: he must be willing to have both the bad *and* the good of self crucified with Christ.

Many people are naturally born with a self that is honest, patient, loving, etc. It is most difficult for them to deliver their *entire self* to death. Quite spontaneously they will retain their honesty, patience and love and allow what is evil in them to be crucified with the Lord. These believers have to be taught by God until they know the utter undependableness of self—whether bad *or* good—before they will obey. Such instruction we find was given to Peter. Before he knew the death and resurrection of the Lord, before he was filled with the Holy Spirit, he had fully convinced himself that he loved the Lord. His heart was good, but did he fulfill the promise he made to the Lord before His crucifixion that "I will lay down my life for thee"? His failure lay in the confidence he had in his own (good) self. He relied on his strong point without truly knowing himself. How very hard to know one's self. We should accept God's evaluation of our self and deliver it to the cross.

If we look at God's judgment of mankind, we shall know more surely of *this* truth: that "there is none righteous, no, not one" (Rom. 3.10). Is this true according to man's view? No, for from the *natural* point of view the world is *not* lacking in righteous people! But God reckons that there is none, because our righteousnesses come from our own self which has been deeply influenced by Adam's nature. How can sweet water come forth from the salty water? "For being ignorant of God's righteousness, and seeking to establish their own, they did not subject themselves to the righteousness of God" (Rom. 10.3). Hence, a self-righteous person is not a righteous one; he is rather a sinner worthy to perish. Only he who has the fullness of Christ is righteous.

Let us look at another place in the word of God. It is a very familiar passage and one which deals with fruitfulness being the result of the death of the good of the self life: "Except a grain of wheat fall into the earth and die," declared the Lord Jesus, "it abideth by itself alone; but if it die, it beareth much fruit" (John 12.24). The Lord includes in this word those who believe in Him. He uses this word to call us to himself. "If any man serve me, let him follow me" (v.26). He does not leave us in the dark as to what this calling is: "He that loveth his life [soul] loseth it [no fruit, no grains in eternity]; and he that hateth his life [soul] in this world shall keep it [he shall not be without fruit] unto life eternal [spiritual life]" (v.25). We can easily discern that the teaching here is about the need of the death of the self life.

Life is most precious. One is willing to lose everything except his life. Yet the calling here is for us to lose our life. This life of self (or soul life) is given by God and is quite legitimate. It is not wrong, yet the Lord calls us to let it die.

What is this life? It is the natural life, the animated life that we share with the living things. Our intellect, will and affection are all controlled by it. For it is the driving force of our entire being. It directs the movements of all the members of our body. It utilizes all the faculties of the soul. Yet this motivating life comes from natural birth, and hence it is not spiritual life. If a believer allows this non-spiritual life to be the main driving force of all his earthly activities, he will lose his life and suffer eternal loss in terms of fruit.

This self life is nonetheless very pretty and attractive. Our Lord illustrates it with the grain of wheat. The outer shell is quite pleasant to look upon. Its color is golden. In spite of its beauty, though, it is useless if it remains as such. The grain of wheat must leave its companions or fall into the ground together with its companions, and die in the place of darkness, obscurity and suffering. In dying, it loses its beauty and all things else, so that it no longer can be exhibited and praised.

If we are really willing to die, and if we in fact do die, we shall lose much praise and applause from men. Our natural beauty will be destroyed. Our intellect, which can conceive fresh teachings and dissertations, will also be dead. We dare not rely on our intelligence as guidance. But then, too, our affection, which can automatically stir up love for the Lord as well as for men, will be dead too. And as a consequence, we no longer allow natural love to induce or impel us; rather, we will let the Holy Spirit pour the love of Christ upon our hearts that we may love with His love. Our natural excitement—that is to say, our emotion—which can create in us a sense of communion with the Lord and give us a sensation of joy, will now be dead in that it will now let the Lord control our excitement so as to grieve or sorrow with the Lord. Although sometimes we may not *feel* the Lord's presence, we remain faithful and normal, unaffected by outside stimuli. What we formerly considered to be profitable we now count as loss for the sake of Christ. As a consequence of our having died to sin with Christ, we henceforth forsake all illegitimate things. But as a consequence of our having been crucified with Christ, we also now forsake those legitimate things of self. Yes, this latter step is much harder: "narrow is the gate, and straitened the way, that leadeth unto life, and few are they that find it" (Matt. 7.14).

How is this death executed? It is the death of the cross. This is exactly what the Lord himself meant by these words which we read in the Scriptures: "But this he said, signifying by what manner of death he should die" (John 12.33). Hence, there is nothing left for us to do but to fall into the ground and die willingly, being glad to die with the Lord and to have fellowship in His cross. Daily maintain this attitude of hating our own life, so that we "shall keep it unto life eternal." We shall bear fruit to eternity, producing many grains. Yet this is not done in a day. If so, it would be relatively easy to accomplish. But recall from the passage quoted above from John 12 that our Lord also used other words most difficult to receive: "hateth his life *in this world.*" As long as we are in this world we need to hate this self life without any let up, recognizing that the self will always try to revive itself.

Let us not despise this word "die." It is not enough simply to be a grain of wheat. To be a regenerated child (see Matt. 13.8,38) is merely to be a newborn baby who can at first do little if anything for God. Neither is it enough only to fall into the ground, for though we may be willing to suffer and to be hidden, we remain as one grain without any increase if we do not die. Death is the final, decisive step. Death is the door to life. Death is the only way to fruitfulness. Death is absolutely necessary. But how many of us are really dead? Death is the cessation of all movements. Once having died, the self can no longer be active. It is the end of man's day. Nonetheless, this death is not something forced, because the Lord declares that this life must be hated. Hate is an attitude, a sustained attitude. For this reason, we must willingly deliver this life to death, fully recognizing its deficiency and hating it with all our heart.

What, though, is the result of the dying of this life? "Much fruit." The reason—the *only* reason—why our Lord cannot use us is because our soul life with its intellect, affection and so forth is of an inferior order which cannot bear any spiritual fruit if we depend on it. Although there are many of what we would consider to be good points surrounding the self life, nevertheless, our Lord Jesus makes clear that only "that which is born of the Spirit is spirit" (John 3.6). The self life with all that it includes can be of no help here. But in the event of our truly delivering ourselves — delivering our life and all that we are *capable* of and all that we *are* — to the cross of Christ, we shall *then* see how God can use us. If we are truly empty of ourselves, the living water of God can and will flow from us without any blockage. And such fruit-bearing as this is out of the ordinary because it shall bear *much* fruit. Yet it all hinges on our death.

Therefore, even as our *self* filled us in the past, let us now let *Christ* fill us; otherwise, we will not have obtained *full* salvation. The turning point in anyone's *full* salvation lies in that one being delivered from self. A self-centered believer is prone to fall into sin. To be wholly dead to sin demands of us that we also die to self. Christ is not only the Savior from our sins, He is also the Savior from our self. To die to the self life is the only pathway to spiritual life. Only God can cause us to die to self; nobody else is able to. But if we are not willing, then this cannot be done even by God himself. The works of the self life are sometimes very subtle, they being covered over or hidden by a spiritual veil. It is beyond the discernment of the believer. So much so that God will have to use outside circumstances to break through such a heavy veil and cause the believer to know his own self. Self-knowledge is extremely rare. We do not know ourselves, at least not until we have been tried by God's hand and been shown the wickedness of our self life. If we have no experience of the death of self, our spiritual life will have little *real* progress. However, if we are willing from now on to let the Spirit of the Lord work the dying of self in us, then we will be able to live out a life in the Spirit.

Let us all say with one accord what our Lord Jesus prayed to His heavenly Father: "not *my* will, but *thine* be done" (Luke 22.42).

2 | Fact, Faith and Experience*

In this present age of grace everything is "by grace"—which means all things are done by God for man. Man is saved without works. For "to him that worketh, the reward is not reckoned as of grace, but as of debt" (Rom. 4.4).

Because God deals with man in grace, there comes "fact." This means everything has already been accomplished by God for the world. Since the thing is done, it is called "fact." Due to it being fact, man has no need to work again for its accomplishment, since the work of God is complete and perfect.

However, the grace of God is righteous grace. Hence, with the presence of fact there is still the need of man's cooperation. What is the nature of this cooperation? It is not that he must add more to the "finished work"

*This article was prepared by the author and published as one of the messages that appeared in a volume he edited, entitled *Spiritual Guide* (1927).—*Translator*

but that he is to acknowledge that what God has done is true. This is "faith." Faith is to confess that all which God has said and done is true. Faith is accepting the fact and taking it as factual.

Moreover, faith is "drawing." I use this word "drawing" in the same sense as drawing from a bank: Someone gives you a check. He has money in the bank. This is a fact. If now you will go and draw out that money, it shows you admit that there is in fact in the bank the amount of money written on the check. In essence, this drawing is done by faith. With faith, you go to draw out. And once it is drawn out, there is money to spend. So that we can say that the money in the bank is "fact"; the drawing out is "faith"; and the spending of the money is "experience" or "favor."

In God's grace there is already the fact of what He has done for man. Yet in man there is still the need of experiencing this fact or entering into this favor. In order to use God's grace experientially you must exercise faith to draw upon the fact accomplished by God. Fact is what God has done. Faith is what man must have. Fact belongs to God whereas experience or favor belongs to man. Faith translates God's fact into man's experience.

And hence, what the Bible shows us is simply "fact — faith — experience."

Looking Collectively

We know that the Lord Jesus Christ is "the Word [who] became flesh" (John 1.14). He is the sum total of all holy virtues. He is the finisher of all great things. His life is the life of God, for He himself is God. On the cross He has accomplished the work of redemption. All who accept in heart Jesus as Savior and Lord are accepted by God, at the very moment of faith, and in the same manner as He has accepted the Lord Jesus. At that time all the holy virtues and perfections of the Lord Jesus come upon the believer. In God's eye the believer's position before Him is the same as that of the Lord Jesus. For God looks at each Christian as Christ. All that is of Christ is reckoned as belonging to the Christian for the sake of his union with Christ. This, then, is the "fact" which the believer inherits before God as a Christian. This fact is what Christ has accomplished for the Christian. Due to the believer's union with Him, all which belongs to Christ belongs in fact to His believer. This is the fact prepared by God, in which the believer himself has absolutely no input.

The Scriptures speak clearly about this fact. The writer of the Letter to the Hebrews uses a distinctively plain illustration to tell us of the fact accomplished for us by God. In 9.15–17 he equates what the Lord Jesus has acccomplished for us with a person who makes a will. In this will and testament, the testator promises to give the "inheritance" to the beneficiary. But the testament in question is not in force as long as the testator lives. But as soon as he dies, the beneficiary can inherit what the testator has promised to give. The Lord Jesus is the Testator. He has died, and therefore all His promises come immediately to us. This is the fact which we receive from Him. Even though it is true that we are not able to possess and enjoy at once all the benefits and supplies of our inheritance, such inheritance is nonetheless ours. It belongs to us, and it is now under our name. It is a fact which cannot be altered. To *have* the inheritance is one thing; to *enjoy* it is another. The former is "fact," the latter is "experience." The fact of our inheritance comes from the Testator, not from ourselves. Fact comes first, then comes enjoyment or experience.

The teaching of this illustration is quite clear. In His death the Lord Jesus gives all His righteous deeds, holy virtues, perfection and victory to us that we might be before God as He himself is and that God might accept us as accepting Him. This is what He has given us. The moment we become Christians all this becomes fact to us. We are in truth as perfect as the Lord Jesus, though in experience we may not be so. Fact means nothing less than all the graces which God has done and given us through the Lord Jesus. Because of our union with the Son of God, all these graces come to us. We may have the fact of our inheritance but may not have the experience of enjoying our inheritance. Fact and experience are vastly different from each other. To-day many believers are rich in fact, because everything which is of God is theirs; yet they are poor in experience since, practically speaking, they have not enjoyed their riches. The elder son mentioned in Luke 15 is a good example. So far as *fact* is concerned, the father in the Lord's parable speaks on this wise: "Son, thou art ever with me, and all that is mine is thine." But in *experience* the elder son complains to his father, saying, "Thou never gavest me a kid, that I might make merry with my friends." He is the son of the rich — such is his position (which is fact); yet it is possible that he has never enjoyed a kid — such is his condition (which is experience).

We should be very clear on the distinction between fact and experience. These two matters speak of two sides: the former is what *God* has accomplished for us, that position which He has given us; the latter is what *we* must practice in order to enjoy what God has given us. Nowadays believers usually go to extremes. Most of them do not know the riches in Christ. They have no idea that all the things the Lord Jesus has accomplished are for them. They plan and plot for God's grace. They exert themselves to their limit to work out many righteousnesses in order to answer God's demands and satisfy the inner urge of their new life. Fewer believers seem to know the grace of God very well. They reckon that because the Lord Jesus has already elevated them to the highest position, they can be fully satisfied and no longer need be concerned about exercising themselves to experience all the graces the Lord Jesus has given them. Both of these attitudes are faulty. To stress experience and forget fact will bring us under the bondage of the law. On the other hand, to emphasize fact and despise experience will cause us to be licentious. A Chrisitan ought to know from the Scriptures what is his noble position in the Lord Jesus, but he ought also to know whether he walks worthily of the calling unto grace under the light of God.

God has already placed us in the noblest position. Due to our union with the Lord Jesus, all which our Lord has accomplished and conquered now belongs to us. This is the *fact* of our position. Our present problem, though, is how we can *experience* all this that the Lord Jesus has accomplished and conquered for us. Between fact and experience there is this vital step of the work of faith — by which is meant translating fact into experience; or in other words, making God's accomplishment become man's practice.

This step of the work of faith means none other than to "possess" and to "manage." The Lord has left His testament to us. Since He now has died, His testament has come into effect. We must not adopt a nonchalant attitude towards it, but must rather rise up to possess our inheritance so that we might enjoy its blessing. We are already the children of God, and therefore all which belongs to Him is now ours (1 Cor. 3.21–23). Let us not be like the elder son in Jesus' parable who has the promise and yet has no enjoyment. This is due to his foolishness and unbelief. He has never asked for it, nor has he ever used it; and hence he possesses none of it. Had he only asked and exercised the right of being a son, a kid would not only have been his, but also, the tens and thousands of sheep would have been his as well!

What we today need is none other than the exercising of faith towards the promises God has given us. *Draw out* by faith what God has provided us in the Lord Jesus. In order to possess and enjoy the inheritance, he who would inherit must take two steps: one, he must believe that there *is* such an inheritance; and two, he must singularly arise to take possession of this inheritance. Disbelieving this inheritance will automatically check him from taking possession of it. Consequently, we must first of all *confess* that God has indeed made Christ to be "unto us wisdom from God, both righteousness and sanctification and redemption" (1 Cor. 1.30 mg.). Whatsoever the Lord Jesus has accomplished and conquered *is* our success and *is* our victory. If we lack in this kind of faith, we not only will be forever deprived of the hope of spiritual experience, but we also will actually offend God inasmuch as we doubt His work. Moreover, we can easily notice that those of the world manage their properties with their fleshly strength. But we must manage our spiritual inheritance with spiritual strength and power—which for us is faith. We must take the step of exercising our faith to appropriate our inheritance in the Lord Jesus, using it and managing it as though this spiritual property were ours.

There is another example in the Scriptures that can serve to illustrate the relationship of fact, faith and experience which we are at present discussing, and this is found in the Old Testament. It is that part of Biblical history which concerns itself with the entering into Canaan of the children of Israel. In the ancient days God had promised to give the land of Canaan to the children of Israel. He had personally spoken to Abraham, to Isaac, to Jacob, and to the tens of thousands of the people who came out of Egypt. So far as God was concerned, He had given the land. He had promised to fight for them and cause them to conquer all their foes. That God had given the land and inhabitants to the children of Israel was already a *fact*. But though there was fact, there was not yet the experience. Though this land was theirs in fact, they nevertheless had not possessed an inch of the land in their experience. It was therefore

necessary that they should "go up at once, and possess
it" since they were "well able to overcome it" (Num.
13.30). Due to their lack of faith, however, they did not
possess the land (experience) even though God had already given it to them (fact). A generation passed away,
and then God said to Joshua, "Every place that the sole
of your foot shall tread upon, to you have I given it,
as I spake unto Moses" (Joshua 1.3). They needed to
possess the land God had promised them by their tread-
ing upon it with the soles of their feet. And these who
were of the next generation did indeed go up, and they
possessed it.

This teaches us the secret of experiencing the perfection of Christ. God has already given us all that Christ
is and *has* and *does*. All which is His is ours. Now it
is for us to experience all of His. Yet for this to become
our experieince there is no other way but to confess that
Canaan is good and by faith to tread with the sole of
our foot upon every inch of the land and to possess
it. God gives, we believe, and then we possess. Fact—
faith—experience.

Definitions

"Fact" is God's promises, God's redemption, God's
work, and God's gift.

"Faith" is how people believe in God, trusting in His
work and redemption, and drawing upon His promises.
Faith is a working attitude and a process which translates God's fact into man's experience.

"Experience" is living a believer's normal life

through faith in God. It is expressing the life of Christ in the believer's daily walk. It is proving the success and victory of Christ by demonstrating practically the fact of God. The histories of those men of God recorded in the Scriptures show forth such a reality in their lives.

All believers, including those who minister the word of God, should know the inter-relation among these three aspects of truth. Otherwise, they will not be clear in their lives as well as in their teachings. They will have difficulties in studying the Scriptures, which to them will appear to be full of contradictions.

I am still fearful that I may not have clearly presented here these principles to be found in the Scriptures. And hence I will try to verify them by applying them to some great truths in the Bible.

We Christians have already believed in the substitutionary death of the Lord Jesus and have experienced the effect of His redemption. Atonement is what the *sinner* experiences. We *Christians* have already been redeemed. Atonement to us is a past experience. We really do not need to mention this, but for the sake of clarifying the relationship with each other of fact, faith and experience, we will touch upon this experience which we already have.

Atonement is a fundamental teaching which we ought clearly to understand. The redemptive work of our Lord Jesus Christ is for the whole world. We have the following Scriptures as proof:

> Behold, the Lamb of God, that taketh away the sin of the world. (John 1.29)
> For God so loved the world, that he gave his only begotten Son. (John 3.16a).

> He is the propitiation for our sins; and not for ours only, but also for the whole world. (1 John 2.2)
> Who gave himself a ransom for all. (1 Tim. 2.6)
> Who is the Saviour of all men. (1 Tim. 4.10c)

By looking at the above passages we know that the redemption of Jesus Christ is for the whole world. Hence, all men have the possibility of being saved. The atonement of the Lord is an accomplished fact.

Nevertheless, *not all* men are saved. This is also revealed in the Scriptures. If one does not know the teaching of "faith" he may surmise that all will be saved — those who indeed believe in the substitutionary death of the Lord as well as those who do not believe. On the surface of things, someone might hold that since Jesus died for the whole world, then all died, regardless whether they believe or disbelieve. This may *appear* rational, but without question it is totally unreasonable; for in anyone taking such a view, the responsibility of the sinner would be completely wiped away and believers would have no need to preach the gospel.

True, the Scriptures do in truth say that Christ died for the whole world, but it also says that those who *believe* shall be saved. The following Scripture verses will prove this:

> That whosoever *believeth* on him should not perish, but have eternal life. (John 3.16b)
> He that *believeth* on him is not judged: he that believeth not hath been judged already, because he hath not believed on the name of the only begotten Son of God. (John 3.18)
> *Believe* on the Lord Jesus, and thou shalt be saved, thou and thy house. (Acts 16.31)

> Even the righteousness of God through *faith* in Jesus Christ unto all them that *believe*; for there is no distinction. (Rom. 3.22)
>
> ... the justifier of him that hath *faith* in Jesus. (Rom. 3.26)
>
> Your sins are forgiven you for his name's sake. (1 John 2.12)

There are many more Scripture verses which can be cited, but the above few quotations sufficiently demonstrate that man must believe. This means that though Christ had died for the world, nonetheless each man needs to draw upon the death of Christ as his death, or else Christ's death is not his. The Bible does say: "For God so loved the world, that he gave his only begotten Son"; but the passage does not stop there, for it continues with: "that whosoever believeth on him should not perish, but have eternal life." For "the living God, who is the Saviour of all men" (1 Tim. 4.10b) sent His Son to the world to die for mankind. Therefore, He is able to be the Savior of all men—"specially of them that believe" (1 Tim. 4.10d), since the believers are those who believe.

Having believed, experience follows. By believing in God's fact, the expression of that fact naturally follows. Please read the following Scriptures;

> He that believeth on him *is not judged:* he that believeth not *hath been judged already.* (John 3.18)
>
> Believeth ... *hath eternal life.* (John 5.24)
>
> Whosoever believeth on him *should not perish, but have eternal life.* (John 3.16)
>
> Being therefore *justified* by faith. (Rom. 5.1a)

Hence all who believe in the salvation which God has

provided for them as fact and who draw upon this salvation shall be saved.

But let us now look at this matter of "died with the Lord" to further explain fact, faith and experience. Believers ought to be fully acquainted with this subject of co-death with Christ just as they are familiar with the subject of redemption.

Fact—when Christ died on the cross, He not only died for sinners but also caused sinners to *die in Him.* He died not only for sin but died also for sinners. That sinners died with Jesus on the cross is God's fact. We have the following Scriptures as proof:

> That one died for all, therefore *all died.* (2 Cor. 5.14b)
> Knowing this, that our old man was *crucified with* him. (Rom. 6.6a)
> We who *died* to sin. (Rom. 6.2)

From these verses (and others could be cited), we gather that in God's eye, believers were crucified with Christ. We may not know this fact, and so we try to crucify ourselves. Daily we try, but daily we fail to be crucified, not knowing we are *already* dead in Christ. What we need to do is not to crucify ourselves but rather to use faith to draw upon His death, reckoning His death as our death. Baptism is the expression of faith as well as a confession. It expresses the fact and confesses it as fact. "Baptized into his death" (Rom. 6.3). This is confessing and appropriating His death by faith.

Although we died, and death and co-death are a fact, we are still commanded by God as follows: "even so reckon ye also yourselves to be dead unto sin." This reckoning is the work of faith and not a looking at ourselves as dead, for this we could not do. We may look from dawn to dusk, but are we able to see ourselves as really dead? The more we look, the more alive we are: how we are prone to sin, we even love to sin. Only by "reckoning" in faith that we are dead *in Christ*—that *His* death is *our* death—do we come to the experience of *co*-death with Christ. From among those mentioned in the Scriptures who had this experience of co-death, Paul is a good representative. He wrote: "far be it from me to glory, save in the cross of our Lord Jesus Christ, through which the world hath been crucified unto me, and I unto the world" (Gal. 6.14); again, "the fellowship of his sufferings, becoming conformed unto his death" (Phil. 3.10); and also, "I have been crucified with Christ" (Gal. 2.20). If believers wish to have the experience of co-death with Christ—to experience it in life—they must not use their own way but use the way of God. This is fact, faith and experience.

The believer has died with Christ on the cross. Do you believe in this fact? Have you accepted this fact and reckoned yourself as dead? Believe, and you will have the experience of co-death, just as Paul believed and experienced. All the teachings in the Scriptures concerning God's dealing with man always follow this procedure: fact, faith and experience.

Whatever God has done is perfect and complete. His way with mankind is to accomplish all the works for men and ask them to draw upon all of His work with faith, without resorting to any human method. For He now treats men with grace, and therefore it does not require men's work (Rom. 4.4). This principle holds

true with respect to such important teachings as sanctification, victory, and so forth.

Sanctification is not our own work, it is done by
God for us: "Jesus also, that he might sanctify the
people through his own blood, suffered without the
gate" (Heb. 13.12); again, "for by one offering he hath
perfected for ever them that are sanctified" (Heb. 10.14).
Sanctification is a completed fact. We are sanctified because Jesus has died. However, in 1 Peter 1.15 we are
commanded: "be ye . . . holy." Why does the apostle
say this? Because in spite of the fact that believers are
already sanctified, this sanctification is only God's fact,
it is not yet the believer's life experience. To be sanctified, it is necessary to draw upon the sanctification
which the death of Jesus has prepared for us. We must
take that sanctification as our sanctification before we
can live a holy life.

The matter of *overcoming the world* follows the
same principle. First is the work which Christ has
accomplished — the fact of God. Jesus said: "I have
overcome the world" (John 16.33). Second is our faith,
for God's word also declares: "this is the victory that
hath overcome the world, even our faith" (1 John 5.4).
And lastly, we draw on the victory of Christ as our own
victory, and so we overcome the world. This third step
is our life experience after we have believed. Fact is
God's work; faith is our trust in God's work; and experience is our having God's work practically in life.

Yet not only sanctification and victory follow this
principle, even all the other major teachings of God's
dealing with men follow it as well.

All God's facts are the works of *God*, not the efforts of *men*. These are not accomplished through the believer's prayer, work, sacrifice, self-denial or plotting. God's facts are done by God himself. All of His enterprises are accomplished *in Christ*. Faith is the only way by which to get to these facts; there is no other way.

Now let us illustrate how far apart from each other are God's fact and man's experience. According to God's fact, the assembly in Corinth was comprised of "them that are sanctified in Christ Jesus" (1 Cor. 1.2). They were the temple of the Holy Spirit (1 Cor. 6.19), even "washed . . . sanctified . . . justified in the name of the Lord Jesus Christ and in the Spirit of our God" (1 Cor. 6.11). But so far as their experience, what do we find? "Nay, already it is altogether a defect in you . . . Nay, but ye yourselves do wrong, and defraud" (1 Cor. 6.7,8); "ye sin against Christ" (1 Cor. 8.12). Why was there this state of affairs among them? It was because they had failed to draw upon the grace (fact) that God had provided for them. And hence such failure was theirs. The lofty position we have in fact is not to be experienced in life through our own attempts, diligence, affliction, pretension or effort. To experience the reality of God's fact for us, we only need to exercise faith to draw on that which the Lord has accomplished for us, taking it as our own. Daily confess what the Lord has done (fact), acknowledge it as truth, and draw it out with true faith. In ordinary times, drawing out means to confess that the work accomplished by Christ is factual and effectual in our life. In times of temptation, however, we must *act* upon this faith as though we have already possessed what He has given us. And thus shall experience happen in our lives.

A believer is more spiritual simply and only because he possesses more spiritual experiences. And these experiences are not self-created but are based on spiritual facts. They are not self-centered, for a believer's spiritual life is wholly dependent on the facts which God has accomplished for him. Fact is the foundation, faith is the process, and experience is the consequence. In other words, fact is the cause, faith is the way, and experience is the effect. A believer's spiritual life experience is but the final result, the final success. In advance of his deep spiritual life is the complete work of the Lord Jesus, which serves as the source. It is absolutely impossible for the believer to attain holiness or victory by his own effort. In order to be holy, victorious and dead to self, he cannot use his own strength but must rather: (1) confess that he is holy, victorious and dead to self in the Lord Jesus; and (2) act as if he *is* holy, victorious and dead to self because he believes that he is united with the Lord Jesus in life. All the experiences one has or wishes to have are already experienced by the Lord Jesus. To draw out by faith is to reckon what the Lord Jesus has as one's own. With the attitude and action of faith, one *uses* what he has reckoned as his own.

Yet in all this, let us not forget the Holy Spirit. How is it that God's fact becomes man's experience through faith? This is because of the work of the Holy Spirit. For when we believe in the fact which God has shown us in the Scriptures and exercise faith to draw upon it, the Holy Spirit will put upon us all the graces which God has accomplished in Christ and cause them to become reality in our lives so that we might experience them personally. Our confessing and our drawing out with faith open the door for the Holy Spirit to work by His adding into our lives that which the Lord has accomplished, thus enabling us to possess practical experiences. All the works of the Holy Spirit are based on God's fact. The Spirit does not accomplish any fact for us, He simply makes the accomplished fact of God real and living in our lives. God has already accomplished fact in the Lord Jesus, and hence we should exercise faith to confess and to draw upon this fact, as well as trust the Holy Spirit to add into our lives what God has done so that we might have spiritual experience.

3 | Witnesses of Christ and the Knowledge of His Resurrection Power*

But ye shall receive power, when the Holy Spirit is come upon you: and ye shall be my witnesses both in Jerusalem, and in all Judea and Samaria, and unto the uttermost part of the earth. (Acts. 1.8)

That I may know him, and the power of his resurrection, and the fellowship of his sufferings, becoming conformed unto his death. (Phil. 3.10)

Resurrection Is the Basis of the Power of the Holy Spirit

Without resurrection there can be no power of the Holy Spirit. The power of resurrection is unto the knowledge of Christ. And the power of the Holy Spirit is unto the testimony of God. To know Christ means

---

*This message was delivered by the author in Hong Kong. The year is uncertain.—*Translator*

to know the power of resurrection; and to know the power of the resurrection of Christ is to know Christ himself. So that in this matter of knowing Christ, knowing the power of His resurrection is a principal factor. Only by our knowing the power of the resurrection of the Lord do we come to the true knowledge of Him. And this power of resurrection is also the power of the Holy Spirit, without which no one is fit to bear witness for the Lord.

Qualification for Being Christ's Witnesses

The biggest problem lies in how much we know Christ. We should not take the filling of the Holy Spirit as the goal. As good as the filling of the Holy Spirit is, that must not be our aim. For the purpose of God is Christ. If we know Him, we naturally are qualified to witness for Him.

To bear witness to Christ is not preaching; neither is it theological knowledge; nor is it Scriptural exposition. We cannot testify for Christ if we base our testimony only on external knowledge. The degree to which we know the power of the resurrection of Christ determines the extent of our declaration before God and men. Without the experience of Philippians 3.10 there can be no witnessing of Acts 1.8. Through the knowledge of the power of resurrection we come to know who Christ is. Naturally we are qualified to be witnesses of Christ, and just as naturally we shall receive the power of the Holy Spirit. There is no need to tarry long for the power of the Holy Spirit, for the power of resurrection is available in a second.

Need to Know Christ in a Real Way

In the southern part of Fukien some young brothers decided to witness for the Lord. I asked them, "What are you going to speak to people about when you testify for the Lord? You may perhaps tell them that Christ is this or that and how many things He has done for you, or you may be able to say only one thing—that Christ is your Savior. Then you have nothing more to say. If such be the case, you are not qualified to be witnesses of the Lord because you do not have much practical knowledge of Him."

Do not think you can witness because you have cleverness and eloquence. What you lack is divine life and the Holy Spirit. Only those who really know Christ can make people live. Do not conclude that because you are saved and possess Biblical knowledge, that because you have eloquence and some good thoughts, you are therefore qualified to witness for Christ. What is essential is your history with the Lord. Many acknowledge that they have shared all that they know of Christ and there is nothing left. This is a shallow knowledge which cannot be taken as the testimony of the riches of Christ. Your recognition of Him as Savior is correct, but this is the minimal condition of any Christian. You ought to have more advanced, richer and more practical experience of the knowledge of Christ so that you can supply what people do not have. What is the use if you can only expound the Scriptures and preach a sermon without a deeper knowledge of Christ?

A brother came to Shanghai and asked me to arrange a preaching opportunity for him. "Your time has not yet come," I told him. "You gave opportunities to three other brothers to speak; give me a chance to speak too," he replied; "if they could occupy the pulpit, why couldn't I? You may sit there and listen to what I say, for I am not inferior to any of them." I therefore politely said to him, "You may be more clever, eloquent, and familiar with the Scriptures, and people may like to hear you speak, but I know you lack one thing which they have, and that is, they have deeper practical knowledge of Christ before God which you do not have. They have many practical experiences, but you have only the experience of being saved without any further knowledge in life." To be a witness of Christ, you must be established on the foundation of the knowledge of Christ. Though you may speak much, you may not necessarily be His witness.

A Life History of Knowing Christ

Suppose a pastor is unregenerated, but he has already graduated from a theological seminary. He knows the teachings covering everything from sinner to salvation. What he has is a theology of salvation, though he has never once definitely received Christ into his heart as Savior. Thereafter a certain church invites him to speak. He preaches a lengthy sermon on the doctrine of salvation. How would you feel if you were one of those sitting there listening? I believe you would hope he would soon be regenerated. Although the sermon is well delivered, he could not say, "Jesus is my Savior." Can we say we have no such danger of this in our midst? It is useless just to preach the word of the cross; we need to know the cross of Christ in our life experience, for thus do we come to the true knowledge of the risen Christ. We must not merely know the doctrine of salvation, we must have our own personal history of salvation. We must not just know the teaching of victory, we must have a history of victory. We must not simply preach about gentleness, resurrection, ascension, the filling of the Holy Spirit, self-denial, self-control and other teachings, we must also have these life experiences in our own spiritual history. Only this will make us truly witnesses of Christ. There is not much use of having mere theologians in the Church.

In one of the local churches it is quite possible that some brother or sister hails from the country place. He has little knowledge, and his thought is not too clear; yet he knows how to commit all things to the Lord and how the Lord is his victory and life. In your conversation with him, you may quote Scriptures, explain the contexts, and interpret many types in the Old Testament. You may also talk with him about law, grace, dispensations, and so forth. What more of life experience or spiritual history are you able to share with him? You may tell him how the Lord has heard your prayers a few times. But the results of your prayers in a whole year may not be equal to the results of his prayers in just one day. Do you think you are more qualified to be the Lord's witness? For, you may say, "What he cannot, I can. I have certain insight which he does not have." I do not mean to say that we have no need of Biblical teaching, clear thinking, or flowing eloquence. What I want to insist upon here is that knowing Christ must be the goal as well as the foundation. It is not as essential to know the teaching of the blood in the Scriptures as to experience the cleansing of the conscience by the precious blood of Christ. The emphasis lies not in whether you are able to preach the word of the cross but in whether you have the experience of delivering self and all that is natural to death on that cross. Do you have the experience of being crucified with Christ?

Someone once asked George Müller the secret of his spiritual life. His answer was: "One day Müller became dead to sin, flesh, self, natural life, and the fame, position and pleasure of the world." As he spoke, he bent himself down till his whole body fell prostrate to the ground. If you say you know Christ, you cannot but have a personal history of knowing Him and the experience of the power of His resurrection. If you speak to people about the message of the cross, are you able to testify that in your daily life, in large and small things, you know how to apply this message of the cross? When you talk to others about the power of the resurrection of Christ, have you yourself experienced this power before? Are you able to testify to that which you naturally do not have but which now is gained through the power of resurrection? When your natural temper is tested beyond endurance, do you experience Christ as your patience? Without such life experience, you are not qualified to be a witness of Christ.

Lost through Death
and Regained in Resurrection

You are able to speak on the teachings of resurrection and ascension, but have you transcended all the things of the earth? Do you have this transcending testimony? If you have not, you lack the reality of the ascended and transcending Christ. Your experience of Him is not deep enough to make you fit as a witness to the resurrection of Christ.

Many brothers came to Shanghai to learn from the church there. They thought that by learning a few external helps they could return home and preach. They could now teach and practice all these external matters such as baptism, the breaking of bread, and holding various kinds of meetings. By having read a little of the Bible and having understood somewhat, they now considered themselves as knowing all. But their self and natural life had never been lost in the death of Christ; therefore, they could not be witnesses to His resurrection.

About three hundred years ago there lived a famous theologian by the name of Bengel. A student of his who was studying the book of Romans ran up to him one day and said, "I have found the doctrine of sin in the Book of Romans." Bengel was at that time reading a book. He jumped up when he heard this word and asked, "Have you found sin in your life and within yourself?" What would this student be profited if he failed to find sin in himself but only found the doctrine of sin in the Book of Romans? What use would there be if he were to speak to others about how they must hate sin, deal with sin, and put no confidence in the flesh, while at the same time he himself would have no experience whatsoever of dealing with sin? How would he be able to deliver people from sin if he himself were not delivered? A sermon without any reality behind it will be preached in vain because the audience will gain nothing from it.

Paul says in the letter to the Philippians to "know ... the power of his resurrection." He does not say, "know the power of the cross," for the cross ends in death and is negative. Resurrection, though, is positive in nature because it is life out of death. It is not mere existence, it is resurrected life. It comes out of death. Have your natural life, eloquence, cleverness and talent been through death into resurrection? Things natural are inherited from your parents. Towards these natural things you ought to have this attitude before the Lord: "I have no use of these things, I do not glory in them, I am willing to let them be lost in death, pass through resurrection, and regained by the Father." If you let them go into death, then after a while—perhaps within three days—to your great surprise God will allow your eloquence to return to your mouth and permit your wisdom and talent to come back to you as well. Nevertheless, they are totally different from what they were before. Your natural good is no longer yours, and you dare not use it anymore. There is a cross that separates it from you. It has been lost in death, but now is regained. And this is resurrection. It is just as in the case of the father of the prodigal son who declared: "my son was dead, and is alive again; he was lost, and is found" (Luke 15.24).

I do not know how much witnesses of Christ have

passed through such experience of "dead and alive," "lost and found." But blessed are those who have indeed experienced it. For thus we begin to know what resurrection is. In our daily life, the more we encounter this dead-alive, lost-found situation, the more we shall experience being dead and alive, lost and found. Such experience is circular in nature.

All of both the good and bad in Adam is concluded in the death of Christ. All of what is the new creation commences in the resurrection of Christ. We ought to stand firm on this resurrection ground, for only in this way can we be fit to receive the power of the Holy Spirit and be witnesses to the resurrection of Christ. It was for this reason that the Lord told the apostles not to depart from Jerusalem, because it would have been a mistake had they gone forth immediately to be witnesses. The apostles had to experience Christ in a practical way before they could receive the power of the Holy Spirit and go forth as witnesses.

As witnesses of Christ, therefore, we need to know more of Christ, more of the power of His resurrection, to know in our experience this loss in death and gain in resurrection. Christ entered into death, but He could not be swallowed by it, for death did not have the power to hold Him. He came out of death. So that whatever is not swallowed up by death is resurrection. The more we experience resurrection, the more that things which belong to us shall be left in the grave, for whatever is natural is finished in death. All which is of Adam lives no more after going through death. Resurrection is the life of the Lord which comes out of death. The sad situation today is that many try to testify to Christ with their natural life, yet few of them witness out of their experiential knowledge of the power of His resurrection. May the natural life be decreased more and more in us and may the resurrection life and its power be increasingly manifested. May the Lord have mercy upon us and be gracious to us. Amen!

4 | Seek for Higher Life and Service*

Jehovah said unto Aaron, Thou and thy sons and thy fathers' house with thee shall bear the iniquity of the sanctuary; and thou and thy sons with thee shall bear the iniquity of your priesthood. And thy brethren also, the tribe of Levi, the tribe of thy father, bring thou near with thee, that they may be joined unto thee, and minister unto thee: but thou and thy sons with thee shall be before the tent of the testimony. And they shall keep thy charge, and the charge of all the tent: only they shall not come nigh unto the vessels of the sanctuary and unto the altar, that they die not, neither they, nor ye. . . . And I, behold, I have

*This article, in the form of a Bible Reading, was prepared by the author in the early days of his ministry. It is unique among the writings of Watchman Nee inasmuch as it was composed in a devotional, expositional literary style. Moreover, it has the distinction of having been set down with Chinese brush in the author's own style of calligraphy. Incidentally, the original draft of the article, still fairly well preserved, was only recently discovered.—*Translator*

taken your brethren the Levites from among the children of Israel: to you they are a gift, given unto Jehovah, to do the service of the tent of meeting. And thou and thy sons with thee shall keep your priesthood for every thing of the altar, and for that within the veil; and ye shall serve: I give you the priesthood as a service of gift: and the stranger that cometh nigh shall be put to death. (Num. 18.1–3,6,7)

And unto the children of Levi, behold, I have given all the tithe in Israel for an inheritance, in return for their service which they serve, even the service of the tent of meeting. . . . For the tithe of the children of Israel, which they offer as a heave-offering unto Jehovah, I have given to the Levites for an inheritance: therefore I have said unto them, Among the children of Israel they shall have no inheritance. And Jehovah spake unto Moses, saying, Moreover thou shalt speak unto the Levites, and say unto them, When ye take of the children of Israel the tithe that I have given you from them for your inheritance, then ye shall offer up a heave-offering of it for Jehovah, a tithe of the tithe. . . . Thus ye also shall offer a heave-offering unto Jehovah of all your tithes, which ye receive of the children of Israel; and thereof ye shall give Jehovah's heave-offering to Aaron the priest. (Num. 18.21,24–26,28)

In this chapter of the Bible, we see three classes of people: (1) the children of Israel, (2) the Levites, and (3) Aaron and his sons. May the Lord teach us needful lessons and edify us through our discussion of these three classes of people so that our lives may be more holy, more closely drawn to Him, and more pleasing to Him.

One—To Be Priests

We know that the children of Israel were chosen from among all the people of the world. The Levites were chosen from the children of Israel. And the priests were chosen from among the Levites. And Aaron was chosen to be the high priest.

In like manner, the Church is called out of the world. The workers in the Church are called out from among the many brothers and sisters. And there is a class of workers who have such intimate fellowship with Jesus Christ that they are called to the highest work with the Lord—which is, to do the work of intercession that our Lord Jesus himself is doing. These people are chosen out of the many workers, and our Lord Jesus himself is their Lord.

Aaron, the high priest of old, is a type of our great and merciful High Priest.

All Christians are priests by God's design: "he made us to be a kingdom, to be priests unto his God and Father" (Rev. 1.6); "ye are an elect race, a royal priesthood" (1 Peter 2.9). Our Lord is now in heaven as the Great High Priest, and we believers are priests according to His word. We do the work which He is now doing— which is, to intercede for men—for we are joined to Him in life. Unfortunately, many believers are totally ignorant of their being priests with the Lord Jesus. They live a soulish life, unseparated from the world.

Some believers are more advanced than the majority of Christians. They know the love of Christ, and they are constrained by His love to offer themselves to do His service. Yet they have not learned how to be quiet in their spirit before the Lord, and thus their works are mainly done according to their natural zeal. They lack the experience of serving as priests with Christ. They are but ordinary workers. Nonetheless, they may have many life experiences and their works may also produce many fruits, even though they have not truly worked with Christ in His work.

People of the world present the largest number; the children of Israel, being chosen out of the world, number less than the total of the world; the Levites number less than the children of Israel; and the priests number less than the Levites.

The Church numbers less than the population of the world; the workers, less than the total of the Church; and the workers who work intimately with Christ, less than the ordinary workers.

As we can see, the number decreases in the scale. Originally, all Christians ought to be priests unto God; but sad to say, they now degenerate into three classes! How few are those who have fellowship with the Lord in the heavenly sanctuary and serve as priests in conjunction with Him! May the Spirit of the Lord touch our hearts and teach us how to seek for the more abundant life and to do the glorious work.

Here let us examine ourselves in the light of the Lord to see whether in life and experience (not in our position in Christ) we are ordinary believers or workers who love the Lord and do His work. If we are workers, what kind of a worker are we? Are we ordinary workers who love the Lord? Or are we those workers who daily bear the burden with the Lord, suffer with Him, and work in secret without human recognition and applause by praying unceasingly before the mercy seat for all men, especially for believers? May God show us wherein we lack, and lead us into His fullness.

Two — Fellowship and Service

Let us look more closely now at the passage from Numbers chapter 18 quoted at the beginning of our discussion.

(1) The children of Israel shall not come near to the tent of meeting (v.22).

(2) The Levites shall keep the charge of the tent of meeting; only, they shall not come near to the vessels of the sanctuary or to the altar (v.3).

(3) Aaron and his sons shall be before the tent of meeting (v.2); they shall keep the charge of the sanctuary and the charge of the altar (v.5); they shall keep their priesthood for everything of the altar and for what is within the veil (v.7).

There are great differences among these three classes of people. God does not allow the children of Israel to enter the tent of meeting because they are not sanctified and offered to Jehovah. The Levites are more advanced than the children of Israel; though they can approach the tent of meeting and keep its charge, they are not permitted to enter the sanctuary. Aaron and his sons are especially selected by God from among the chosen ones; they are privileged to draw near to God to fellowship with Him and to do the most holy work of intercession.

The children of Israel are born to be the children of Israel; the Levites are born to be the Levites; and Aaron and his sons, too, are born to be themselves. There is no transference or change as they might possibly wish.

However, we believers who are redeemed by the precious blood are made priests unto God. The children of Israel had their classification determined at birth. But great is our privilege who are born of the Spirit to be priests.

How sad that many believers do not know this privilege and abandon it. According to design, all believers are priests; and as priests we all can hold sweet fellowship with God, sense at all times the reality of His presence, and plead for sinners at His throne of grace.

Yet due to the fact that believers forsake their privilege, there are now in the Church three classes of believers. This refers not to their position before God, it only refers to their experience in life. One class of believers is the merely saved Christians; another class are workers who can only preach and teach; and a third class (few there be) are functioning priests who join themselves to the Lord and pray according to God's heart for the things the Lord would have accomplished.

What the Levites do are seen by all, for their office is to keep the charge of the tent of meeting and to do its service (Num. 18.3,6). Their works are external, therefore visible to all.

The tent of meeting represents the incarnated Christ.

The service of the Levites as recorded in Numbers chapters 3, 4, 7 and 8 is to carry the tent of meeting, together with all the vessels in it. So their labor is visible and sometimes may receive praise and glory from men.

But those who serve as priests of God do not have such kind of notoriety. Their work is hidden, for they dwell in the secret place of the Most High. May God our Father create in us a desire to be near to His heart, enabling us to forsake all the excitement, glory and praise of the world and to fellowship with our Father incessantly by living in His presence and praying for all men.

A further word can be said about those who serve God in the sanctuary: they have no social interaction. Apart from the fellowship they have among themselves, they are separated from the world. If anyone wishes to serve God with all his heart and to live for Him, he cannot occupy himself with many social relationships and functions. He ought to spend more time in fellowshipping with the Father who loves us, and in working for Him.

The sanctuary is not a spacious place, although it is large enough for us to commune with the Lord. The sanctuary is dark because the sunlight cannot penetrate it, and therefore we must walk by faith. The sanctuary is tranquil, solitary, secret and concealed, unseen and unknown by men. Are you willing to be there? To serve our God in *this* fashion is costly, but the love of Christ ought to constrain us into forsaking all and presenting our bodies for His service alone.

Our Lord has died for us and is now praying for

us in the heavenly sanctuary. Should we not be where
He is and join ourselves together with Him?

The blood of Christ has already cleansed us so that
we might function as priests. Let us therefore come
boldly before Him.

Do take note that the priesthood is God's gift (Num.
18.7). It is a super-glorious service. How we should im-
itate Christ in doing this glorious work!

Three — Responsibility

There is more to be found in chapter 18 of Numbers.
Here we shall deal with this matter of responsibility.

(1) The children of Israel bear their own sin (v.22).

(2) The Levites bear the iniquity of the sanctuary
(v.1) as well as the iniquity of the tent of meeting (v.23).

(3) The priests bear the iniquity of the sanctuary
with the Levites but also bear the iniquity of the
priesthood (v.1).

God gives responsibility to each according to his
position in His work. Today such position is not viewed
through the eyes of the Church but viewed through the
eyes of God. To those whom God judges to be more
spiritual and talented He puts more responsibility upon
their shoulders. For to whomever He gives more, of
them He requires more (see Luke 12.48b).

Man's position in the work is decided by his life.
This is because God cannot and will not use an un-
holy person. He cannot use one who is not fully consecrated and is not obedient to His will. Whoever
pleases Him in life He will use. He looks at what a per-

son is, rather than at what a person does. The more humble one is at God's feet, the more useful he is in His hand. God's work is holy, therefore He requires a holy person to do it.

Man's holiness is not derived from his own works but from his appropriation of the experience of the Lord as his own experience. The more he appropriates of Christ, the stronger his life becomes. To him who appropriates more of Christ, more responsibility in the work of the Lord is laid upon him. He who does not take Christ by faith is not able to do effective work for Him. How can he preach the word of salvation if he has not received Christ? Where does he obtain the grace to kneel before God and plead for men if not from Christ?

All who appropriate Christ as their sanctification are today's Levites. All who are separated from the world unto God are qualified to be today's Levites.

All who appropriate Christ and join with Him, drawing near to God through Him at all times and communing with God; all who, under whatever circumstance, wherever they are, and whoever they meet, are able to know the presence of God in faith and in experience; all who are always led by the Holy Spirit in receiving prayer burdens and faithfully executing them before God—they are the real priests of today.

God is now seeking for people whom He can use. How few there are! Shall we too fail God?

God is now calling us to bear greater responsibility and to maintain closer fellowship with Him. For the sake of loving the Lord we should joyfully receive His call to His service. Let us respond by saying: Lord, may

Your will be done: in spite of the tremendous responsibility of the sanctuary and the priesthood, we are willing to bear it.

To take up responsibility is to bear the iniquity.

Unfaithfulness in service incurs penalty, and the penalty is "death." Please take note that I believe that whosoever believes in the Lord is once saved and forever saved. No one can condemn them for their sins anymore. But I also believe that believers as saved people will receive judgment over their works. It is not a judgment of eternal life or eternal perdition but a judgment of reward or loss.

So the "death" here does not mean perdition; rather, it signifies reproach. At the coming of the Lord, all unfaithful workers will suffer reproach.

The work of God is holy, therefore "death" is used here to indicate the seriousness and solemnity of this work. He calls us to work with Him. Is not this amazing? Although He is most holy, most glorious, high above all and beyond compare, He nonetheless treats us with patience and bears our burdens daily. In spite of the fact that we are weak, fail much, and lack an understanding of His heart, He is mindful of us, is slow to anger and is full of mercy. Our Lord is truly our beloved Lord! Hallelujah!

We know His mercy, but we also need to know His terror.

We must not mock Him, for He is the Greatest.

Because the work we do is God's work, therefore Paul declares: "Henceforth let no man trouble me: for I bear branded on my body the marks of Jesus" (Gal.

6.17). This is the meaning of "a stranger shall not come nigh unto you" (Num. 18.4).

May God cause us to sense the greatness of our responsibility and the solemnity of our relationship to Him so that we may be sanctified in the fear of God.

All our works and responsibilities are for God. He has no delight in reproaching us, yet He cannot but punish sin. Happily, intercession — as indicated in Numbers 18 — can turn away His wrath (v.5). We ought to intercede more for people.

Though the children of Israel can worship God, they nonetheless have no part in conducting worship and doing God's work.

Ordinary believers may worship God, but they are as visitors to Him.

The Levites are closely related with the priests: "thy brethren also, the tribe of Levi, the tribe of thy father, bring thou near with thee, that they may be joined unto thee, and minister unto thee" (v.2); and, "they shall be joined unto thee" (v.4).

The Levites work for God, and Aaron and his sons the priests also work for God; therefore, they are especially joined together. This is why many of their works are shared with each other.

Workers who function as God's priests not only intercede for people, they sometimes also come out to deliver God's message to men. Workers as Levites are mere messengers of God. These two classes have something in common as well as something different about them. So, they are largely joined. (A great preacher must be a great pray-er; his preaching is supported by his praying.)

Those who do not draw near to the tent of meeting may not possess great holiness. They seem to be free to do what they will. Their daily lives are only slightly restricted by some principles of Christ. They are able to enjoy the pleasures of this world and seek after its glory. They may have both morality and prosperity in the world.

It is more exacting for people who are wholly consecrated and serve in the sanctuary of the Lord. They take up responsibility on behalf of the Lord. Slowly and patiently they walk, as it were, on their knees with Jehovah. They make the mind of Christ their mind, thus being humble and obedient. They are so filled with the love for mankind that their hearts are saddened at seeing people perishing and they sigh before God under the burden of His plan.

To serve in the sanctuary is something seldom seen by men. Except for God, no one sees them. They receive neither glory nor praise from men. They shut the door and pray in secret. They are rewarded in secret. In a place which is unknown to men they see God's face, hear His voice and walk with Him. They serve in the dark and lonely place within the veil.

Do not impulsively decide to be priests.

To be an ordinary believer, you can have blessings in this world as well as eternal life in the world to come. Why not enjoy these two worlds? Lift up your eyes and observe how such believers do live indeed in pleasure and enjoyment! (I do not blame them.) How good is their dwelling, their food and their clothing. This road they travel is admittedly very broad. So unless you have

counted the cost to yourself, then you should not out-
right say you will not walk in it.

It is harder for the Levite-type workers than for the
ordinary believers just described. As preachers and
evangelists, the Levite-type workers roam about the rural
places, seeking with the Lord those who are lost. Sometimes they are scorched by the sun, sometimes they are
drenched by the rain. The weather may be hot and the
road slippery, yet they set their hearts as flint in spread-
ing the gospel. Is it not, because of these circumstances,
a much harder way? They cannot enjoy what ordinary
believers indulge in. Though they do find some periods
of repose, nevertheless, those times are few and far
apart.

And for the people who function as priests, there
is even more self-abandonment in order to see God.
They remain silent even though they have lost all earthly
blessings.

Let us recall how our loving Lord has died for us.
He delivers us from the power of sin as well as saves
us from future punishment. Let us therefore live before
His presence, walk and work together with Him through
this great and terrible wilderness.

In the name of God the Father, I beseech you this
day: seek for the higher life—which is the priestly life,
and for the higher service—which is the priestly service. I do not know who is willing hereafter to put his
hand on the plow and not look back at the world.
Count all things as dross in order to gain Christ. Wholly
and unconditionally obey the Lord. Be humble and pli-
able in His hand. Be ever ready to be sent by Him to
far or near, to a gregarious or solitary situation, ac-

cording to His will. Be content to be lonely in spirit and quiet in body, rescuing lost sheep with tears and knees, suffering together with Him. In spite of adverse talk, misunderstanding, hostility, despising, disgrace or mockery, such hearts will turn heavenward and be tuned to the heart of the One who sits upon the throne. Being moved by the Spirit, they too will cry out, "Father, forgive them; for they know not what they do" (Luke 23.34). They do not regard prayer as too slow a way, for they always trust in the Everlasting Arms.

Glory is ahead of us. May the Lord strengthen us in obtaining it.

Four — Inheritance

Let us now turn to the matter of inheritance — again looking into Numbers 18.

(1) The children of Israel have an earthly inheritance (cf. vv.20 and 23).

(2) The Levites have the tithe as their inheritance (vv.21,23). And they must tithe their tithe (vv.26,28).

(3) Aaron has no inheritance because the Lord is his portion (v.20).

We are today on earth as strangers and sojourners. The day is fast approaching when we shall be called to heaven. Why, then, seek for more inheritance on earth to increase our burden? I travel much, and the most distressful task of a traveler is to take care of the luggage. The more luggage the more troublesome the task. So let us, as heavenly pilgrims, carry less baggage. With faces set towards the heavenly Jesusalem, we do not know when we shall be called to lay aside the tent and go.

The Levites have cities to dwell in (Josh. 14.4), wherein they may find much comfort and rest. The priests do not have any such city (read carefully Joshua 21).*

Though like the priests the Levites have no inheritance among the children of Israel (vv.20,23,24), they nonetheless have cities which the priests do not have.

Let us live in this world as homeless persons, with not even a place to lay our heads; and yet let us feel at home everywhere. For God is with us, and the Lord himself is our inheritance and our portion. Having Him we are satisfied. Apart from Him we have no desire for any other possession. He is our all. We look to Him alone. We long after Him and after His pleasure. We serve Him and no one else.

Compared with the earthly possessions of the children of Israel, the Levites appear as though having nothing. What they do have comes directly from the Lord.

Each time the children of Israel come to the Lord, they have something to offer. They offer bullocks, sheep, or sometimes gold and silver. They have the appearance of being the most zealous of believers, the most willing to offer. But what they offer is mostly the surplus. Though they seem to have offered much, they

---

*Here the author is found making a fine distinction; namely, that the priests did not receive any cities as *priests* but only as Levites.—*Translator*

have not offered all. (Of course, the people of today who belong to the self-centered class are far worse in this regard than even these Old Testament believers.)

Let us offer till there is nothing more to offer — for this is perfect offering.

Besides their various responsibilities and services, the Levites live a city life marked by social interaction and repose.

But the priests, apart from the tranquil and solitary life they lead in the tent of meeting, have no other life. In that restricted area they seek God's pleasure, and they are constantly occupied with the Father's business. They often hear His voice and commune with Him. The world is shut outside, for they live in the presence of God.

Let us take God as our satisfaction, with distraction neither from city life nor inheritance.

Owing to the fact of no inheritance, we are restricted in many things. But for the sake of the Lord we are more than willing to be so.

Let us come forth to teach people on behalf of God. Let us enter in to pray to Him on behalf of men.

Nothing is for our own selves!

Five — Food

Finally, as to the matter of food and sustenance for livelihood, there is much to be learned from Numbers 18 on this subject as well.

(1) The children of Israel receive nine-tenths, or ninety percent, of all the food of the nation (vv.21,24).

(2) The Levites receive one-tenth or ten percent of the food, but they must give as a heave-offering one-tenth of what they receive (v.26), and thus they are left with but nine percent for themselves.

(3) Aaron and his sons have only one percent.

Some Christians possess more on earth. They are always rich and full. May the Lord keep our hearts from being jealous of them or from admiring them.

They have the ability to give much while we have little to give.

They are fed well and clothed well.

If they fail in tithing, the Levites will become hungry. The Lord will suffer and the Levites too will suffer. Whenever people fail the Lord in this regard, some are bound to suffer.

The portion of the Levites is ten percent; still, they must offer one-tenth of what they receive. How hard this is! Is not their portion already small? Have they not offered themselves to serve the Lord? They have hardly enough to live by, and why, then, must they offer again?

But this is a heave-offering to the Lord (v.26). Is there anything impossible for the sake of the Lord? Even if the demand is greater, it is still worth it to meet that demand.

What one part of the ten percent is to be given to the Lord? The very best! (see vv.29,30,32)

The best is to be offered to the Lord for He is worthy of the very best.

The result—"then it shall be reckoned unto the Levites as the increase of the threshing-floor, and as the increase of the winepress" (v.30).

The one percent is received by the Lord as their all. Although they offer only one-tenth, the Lord accepts their heart and reckons it as their all. This is because they are willing to do what the Lord requires. How gracious is the Lord.

There is a reward attached, and the reward is: "Ye shall eat it [the leftover after the "best" has been offered] in every place, ye and your households" (v.31). The Lord owes no one. It is therefore not in vain to labor for the Lord.

The heave-offering is unto the Lord. Yet what belongs to the Lord is given to Aaron and his sons (vv.26, 28,8). The Lord's portion is the portion of the priests. What the Lord has, the priests have; what the Lord does not have, the priests likewise do not have. For they are deeply joined to the Lord. What a blessing this is! Let us lay down all that is earthly and partake in the "have" and "have not" of the holy Father. How noble this is! May the Lord at this time lift our spirits by His Spirit far above this world and unite us with the heart of the One who sits upon the throne. May the Lord cause us to know today the joy of union with Him.

Heave-offering—

(1) "My heave-offerings" (v.8). The heave-offering is the tithe which the Levites offer out of their received tithe. It is Jehovah's portion.

(2) "Have given thee" (v.8). The Lord gives His portion to the priests. Does the Lord dare to trust us with His things? "Jesus did not trust himself unto them, for that he knew all men" (John 2.24). Are we worthy of His trust? Are we faithful?

(3) "Unto thee have I given them" (v.8). How great is His grace! Is all that is offered to Him ours? Who can tell the boundless grace that all which is His is ours! "Even all the hallowed things" (v.8). All, all, *all* is ours! His riches are all ours! "Son, thou art ever with me, and all that is mine is thine" (Luke 15.31). How blessed is this knowledge. Whatever is the Lord's is the priest's. This is perfect union.

(4) "Shalt thou eat thereof" (v.10). What we eat becomes bone of our bones and flesh of our flesh. It becomes part of us. To "eat" implies to "appropriate." Since the Lord has given, let us appropriate so that what He gives will become part of us. The first three points above refer to the fact of union. This matter of the heave-offering points to the experience of union.

To whom given —

(1) "By reason of the anointing" (v.8). Those who are filled with the Holy Spirit can alone be united with the Lord in fact and in experience. How our Lord is always anxious to fill us with His Spirit. It is our lack of consecration and obedience which hinders His filling. Let us realize that we ought to obey fully and constantly so that today we too might have this extraordinary blessing.

(2) "And for thy sons" (v.9). This refers to those who are joined to the Lord. There must be union with Him positionally before there can be union experientially.

(3) "Every male" (v.10). This suggests manhood. "Quit you like men, be strong" (1 Cor. 16.13). The strong alone can keep the reward.

(4) "Every one that is clean" (v.11). The Lord is holy,

therefore we must be holy. Only the pure in heart and clean in hand may experience God's special gift.

What God has given us is the best (v.12). May we receive His gift with praises.

(*Note*: As we have seen, the Levites number less than the total of the children of Israel; and the priests number less than that of the Levites. We know that one hundred percent belongs to the children of Israel. If they should fail in giving their tithes, then the Levites and the priests will have nothing. Unfortunately, we know from our reading of the prophets that the children of Israel actually failed in their tithing, thus reducing the Levites and the priests to poverty.)

Six—A Request

Three ways are now placed before you; which one will you choose? Will you be an ordinary believer, a common worker, or one of God's workmen who always sees His face and works with Him in establishing other believers as well as saving sinners?

5 | Who Are We?*

> They said therefore unto him, Who art thou? that we may give an answer to them that sent us. What sayest thou of thyself? (John 1.22)
>
> Wherefore I shall be ready always to put you in remembrance of these things, though ye know them, and are established in the truth which is with you. (2 Peter 1.12)

Today we would deal with one focal question: Who are we? Why are we here? In the past we had rarely touched upon this matter because we felt embarrassed

*This message was delivered at the Third Victory Conference held at Shanghai, China, in January 1934. It will be of interest to readers of Watchman Nee to note that it was at this same Conference that the author's unusual messages on the general theme of "God's Plan and the Overcomers" were also given. A translated synopsis of these messages, published in 1977 under the same title, is available from Christian Fellowship Publishers.—*Translator*

about mentioning it. Nevertheless, we are constantly being asked by people, "What are you?" At various times people have denominated us as the Revivalists, the Little Flock, the Association of Christian Magazine, and so forth. For this reason I am compelled today to say a few words on this subject.

First of all, let me declare that we are not anything. We are not a new denomination, a new sect, a new movement, or a new institution. We neither join any party nor create any party. Except for the special calling and special burden God has given, we have no reason to be here. We are here simply and only because God has called us with a special calling.

In 2 Peter chapter 1 verse 12, which we read at the beginning, we find this expression: "the truth which is with you." In the original this is rendered, "the present truth"—which may also be translated as "today's truth." Now, what is today's truth? All truths are recorded in the Scriptures. There is no truth which is not found in the word of God. Though all are documented in the Bible, many of them have nonetheless been buried in God's word and hidden from mankind because of the foolishness, unfaithfulness, irresponsibility and disobedience of men. These truths have indeed been there, but men could not see or touch them. But at what God considers to be "the fullness of time," He will release some truths during a certain period and cause them to be revealed once again.

These recovered truths are not newly created by God, nor are they a brand new discovery of men. No, these truths are not human invention, they are merely rediscovered by men. Throughout the past ages God had revealed various truths. But at certain particular times thereafter He has allowed men to *re*-discover them. This fact may be clearly observed in the history of the Church.

For example, in the sixteenth century God raised up Martin Luther and caused him to see what is "justification by faith." Luther became God's chosen vessel in manifesting this truth. Yet this did not mean that before Luther there had never been such a truth as justification by faith, for as a matter of fact it had been in existence a long while before the Reformer. As it turned out, however, Luther became the one who knew this truth the best. And thus this teaching became "the present truth" for that period of re-discovery in sixteenth-century Germany.

Every worker of the Lord needs to inquire before God as to what is today's truth. We need to ask Him, "O God, what is the present truth?" Although in the Bible there are many cardinal and weighty truths, we nonetheless need to discern what is today's truth which God wishes us to know. We must not only know general truths, we need to clearly know also what is God's truth of today.

Since the commencement of the sixteenth century, God has been recovering various truths. This particular century was the time of the Reformation, a great turning point in religious history. This is not meant to imply, however, that before that century there had been no recovery work of God. As a matter of known fact, there were a number of recoveries of God's truth before that time. Even so, it has been preeminently since the sixteenth century that there have been major recoveries.

In our discussion today, therefore, we will view Church history from the beginning of the sixteenth century in four major periods: (1) the time of the Reformation; (2) the time immediately after the Reformation from roughly the sixteenth to the eighteenth centuries; (3) the time of the nineteenth century; and (4) the current twentieth century.

Let us first look more closely at Luther's Reformation. Martin Luther was raised up by God and given light for the Church to return to the Biblical truth to be found in the Book of Romans. Today a number of people criticize Luther's work as having not only religious but also political overtones. These critics consider his movement to have been significantly a political one, and such criticism is not without some merit. But in reading his diary, writings and letters, I can nonetheless clearly discern that his motive and goal were good: they were essentially spiritual in nature. His best achievement was in recovering the truth of "justification by faith." This was something particularly special with him.

Yet it is quite obvious that God did not recover all needful truths through Luther. What was recovered through him was but the truth of justification by faith, Luther's work not having changed the Church completely for the better. For instance, the German Reformer recognized the National Church and acknowledged the Church as belonging to the State. This was because in this particular area, Luther had little or no light. And as a consequence, very soon thereafter there emerged the Lutherans who followed him and the Lutheran Church that became a National Church in Germany and elsewhere. Luther did once say that the

Church is not governed by the politics of the State, yet he also confessed that this matter of Church government is a transient thing, it belonging to "the outer court," it being something temporary and thus not a matter of "the sanctuary." We learn from all this that Luther made no thorough effort to solve this problem. God allowed this matter of Church government to remain an unresolved issue during the time of Luther.

Notwithstanding the lack of successful recovery in this area, however, the truth of the justification by faith was definitely re-discovered and fully recovered for the Church. Through Martin Luther God dug out this buried truth from the debris of human traditions and decrees and made it known, recognized and spread abroad to all men. Consequently, people who were born at that time needed to propagate this teaching and to persuade men with this truth; otherwise, they would not have been deemed to be God's faithful workers during that particular Church age.

Following the noting of this recovery by Luther, we would now turn our attention to the second main period under discussion—lasting roughly from the early sixteenth century to the eighteenth century. In the year 1524 there emerged a group of believers in Germany known as the Anabaptists (meaning "baptize again") who believed in believer's baptism and that by immersion. They succeeded the (Czechoslovakian) Lhotka brethren of an earlier time who had advocated believer's baptism. It needs to be mentioned that, prior to their time, both the Roman Catholic Church and the Lutheran Church practiced infant baptism by sprinkling. This new group called Anabaptists now not only preached "justification by faith"; they also took a further step of recovery in advocating the baptism of all those believers who have been justified by faith. Later on, when the Anglican Church was formed in England, these Anabaptists—both foreign-born and native-born—took a further position by telling people there that the Church should not be mixed with politics. Because of this, they were persecuted and exiled from England.

Twelve years later, in 1536, God raised up John Calvin. During this special time period he was the greatest vessel of God. But Calvin, too, was persecuted wherever he went, first in Switzerland, then in Germany, and finally in Scotland where, through his efforts and those of others, the Scottish Presbyterian Church was formed.

Towards the middle of the sixteenth century and on into the beginning of the seventeenth, there took place the formation and development of the Anglican Church of England. This was the commencement of the English National Church. Though members of this National Church had shaken off the influence of Rome, they nonetheless joined in with British politics. And as a consequence, dissenters within the Anglican Communion arose to voice their opposition. They opposed the concept of a National Church; they judged that the Church must not be controlled by the State; and they further advocated the clear separation of the Church from politics. In spite of the fact that these English dissenters courageously pointed out the error of a National Church, they nonetheless did not return to the entire teaching of the New Testament.

Meanwhile back in Germany, God was raising up Philip Jacob Spener. In 1670 he became a Lutheran pastor in Frankfurt. At that time the Lutheran Church had fallen into a religion of forms. While Spener was studying the Scriptures, he discovered that the Church was full of human ideas that were forbidden by God. He was convinced that believers should return to the teachings of the New Testament. And hence Spener began to lead people in practicing the teaching of First Corinthians 14. In his meeting people were taught to follow the leading of the Holy Spirit instead of keeping the rituals of traditions. But such a practice did not last very long.

In 1732 the earliest missionary association was formed, and was the work of the Moravian Brethren. The term Moravians had reference to people who hailed from the place called Moravia in East Central Europe. They were the first group of Christians to go out to evangelize the world. Eighty-five out of a given hundred of them went abroad as missionaries. All this began with a brother by the name of Christian David. When about twenty-two years of age, he was born again of the Spirit of God. Prior to his rebirth in Christ he had sought for the way of salvation in many places without receiving the experience. Finally, one day he found the door of salvation. And in returning to his old home in Moravia, David set about proclaiming this truth of new birth in Christ. God used him to do a great work. Following revival there came persecution for him and others. Driven out of his home to distant Saxony, David made the acquaintance there of Count von Zinzendorf. At that time Zinzendorf was only twenty-two years old and a member of the nobility in a small kingdom. Now due to the persecution of the Moravians, brethren were seeking out a refuge, and Zinzendorf eventually welcomed them to his estate. There the Moravian Church (or the *Unitas Fratrum*, Unity of Brethren, the official Latin title) was further consolidated. By a hillside in Saxony on Zinzendorf's estate they built their settlement, and gradually, other persecuted Christians belonging to various denominations everywhere fled there and settled down.

A negro slave by the name of Anthony came to visit Herrnhut (the name of this exile settlement in Saxony) and told the settlers in person about the longing of the people in the West Indies for the gospel. The exiled brethren felt the need of preaching the gospel to these slaves. Through the casting of lots, Leonard Dober was chosen to go to the West Indies for the sake of the gospel. An older man, David Nitschmann, accompanied him on the journey. This was the first attempt at foreign missionary work and launched the earliest missionary association ever to be formed, which happened in the year 1732. Thereafter, missionaries were to go forth from their midst in rapid succession until the Moravian Church became the most effective missionary group at that age. Its believers spread to many corners of the whole world.

Somewhat earlier there had emerged a new rediscovery among the Roman Catholics. A group of spiritual people was raised up, with Miguel de Molinos as one of the leading personages. He was born in 1640 and died in 1697. Molinos was the author of a treatise entitled "Spiritual Guide" that instructed people how to deny self and how to die with Christ. This book soon became the most influential writing of that day. Madame Guyon was his contemporary. Born in 1647, she came to have a deep understanding of how to be united with the will of God and how to forsake self. Her autobiography is a very good and quite significant book. She died in 1717.

Besides these two Catholics there was also Archbishop Fénelon (1648–1715). He cooperated with Madame Guyon and was most willing to suffer for the Lord. Through these people God was able to release many spiritual teachings. During that period people of the deeper spiritual life were mostly to be found in the Catholic Church, whereas the Protestants laid stress mainly on the truth of justification by faith.

Mention should also be made of Gottfried Arnold (1666–1714) who wrote many books and discoursed on the matter of the Church. He reckoned that the Church of his time had departed from the truth. In his estimation a right Church could only be established by returning to the New Testament ground.

Here, then, can be seen two streams: the first flowed from such people as Molinos, Madame Guyon, Fénelon, and others; the second stream flowed from people represented by Gottfried Arnold. From a reading of the *Spiritual Torrents* of Madame Guyon we can conclude that she was indeed a very spiritual person. And as to what Arnold recovered for the Church, it mainly concerned itself with the external, he advocating a return to the New Testament ground.

These two streams later merged and became what came to be termed as the Philadelphia societies or churches of the 1700's. "Philadelphia" in the Scriptures connotes brotherly love. As we read the second and third chapters of the Book of Revelation, we come to understand that the Protestant Church as represented by the local church at Sardis comes out of the Roman Catholic Church as represented by the local church at Thyatira. And thus what we find in the church at Sardis does not reflect a full recovery of the truth of God.

Nevertheless, as the two streams just described merged and became like the local church at Philadelphia mentioned in Revelation chapter 3, this so-called Philadelphia church began to mushroom in various locations. But unlike what other sects or denominations usually did, these local expressions did not ask people to leave their original sects or denominations; those believers involved merely began to assemble themselves. From 1670 onwards they had their testimony in Leeds, Belford, and many other places in England. They were the strongest and most powerful witnesses to this aspect of God's truth in the eighteenth century. Even Zinzendorf, who was still living at the time, had made an unsuccessful attempt to absorb this movement into the Moravian Church.

Moving ahead, at the commencement of the eighteenth century a great revival broke out in England. In 1729 at Oxford University, the two Wesley brothers were being raised up by God. They and their companions were labeled "the Holy Club." Through them a large and significant stream of revival was brought in. Unbeknown at the time, this actually served as the beginning of the Wesleyan (or Methodist) Church. These two brothers were the principal figures dominating the eighteenth century. Before John Wesley was saved he had striven earnestly after good works. He even later sailed to America to preach, although he himself was yet unsaved. John Wesley later testified that though he had heard of the truth of justification by faith, he could not understand it. Quite sovereignly of God a Moravian brother crossed Wesley's path, who helped him and advised him by declaring: "Preach faith till you have it; and then, because you have it, you will preach faith." It was not long after this that Wesley did indeed experience salvation through the new birth. And once saved, these two Wesley brothers immediately began to spread the good news everywhere. At that time, however, preaching was required to be done in church buildings and certainly never on the streets, for the Anglican Church maintained that the holy word could only be proclaimed in the holy place. But the Wesley brothers and their emerging colleague George Whitefield dared to preach in the open air and led multitudes to Christ.

Now the focal point of John Wesley's teaching was sanctification. And as a part of his emphasis on sanctification, an erroneous teaching concerning the eradication of sin began to develop and be identified with him, although he himself did tell people that sanctification was by faith.

It was after the death of the Wesleys that the greater movement of foreign missions commenced and flourished. One of the first missions to be formed in this period was the London Missionary Society which at first was non-denominational in character but later on became Congregationalist. In 1799 the Church Missionary Society (C.M.S.) was formed. It was the foreign missions arm of the Anglican Church. The missionary organization of the followers of the Wesleys (known as the Wesleyans) was further extended and eventually became known as the Methodist Church.

To sum up this second period of Church history under discussion, we may say that the reform which marked the sixteenth century was general in nature, whereas that of the eighteenth century was not so general. The earlier reforms influenced not only the spiritual world but the political and social worlds as well. Not so, though, with the latter reforms, which had their focus *mainly* in the spiritual realm.* The most notable of the reform movements that flowered during the eighteenth century was the testimony of "the Philadelphia church," inasmuch as it gathered up all the principal recoveries of the recent past up to that time.

Now let us turn to the nineteenth century. In this period we have an even fuller recovery. First of all, let us review the recovery that has come to be associated with the name of John Nelson Darby.

In 1827 at Dublin, Ireland, a group of believers, among whom were Edward Cronin, Anthony Norris Groves and others, saw that many things in the Church were dead, lifeless and mere rituals. They sought the Lord to show them the Church of God's thought as revealed in the Bible. After much prayer and fellowship they felt they should meet according to the principles

---

*Nevertheless, it should be pointed out that a number of scholars have claimed that the Wesleyan revival of the eighteenth century did indeed have a significant social impact on British society for good.—*Translator*

given in 1 Corinthians 14. They thus began to break bread in a brother's home. Not long afterwards an Anglican curate by the name of John N. Darby joined them in their meetings and expounded God's word among them. Later on, many well-known Bible expositors began to appear in their midst—men such as William Kelly, C. H. Mackintosh, John Newton, John G. Bellett, and others. Through my own reading of their writings I myself received much light on the oneness of the Body of Christ as well as on the errors of denominationalism. The Church, they argued, should not be organized according to human ideas; she should instead be led directly by the Holy Spirit. Today, as in their day, we witness in the organized Church much of human traditions and ideas and little of the direct guidance of the Holy Spirit. This certainly is not according to God's heart desire. In the will of God the Church ought not to be controlled by men but be governed by the Holy Spirit. All who belong to the Lord should learn to be led by the Spirit of God instead of following the dictates of men. All these insights were re-discovered by the Brethren, as they later came to be known.

The Brethren made many other discoveries as well. These were such matters as the prophetic interpretations surrounding the coming millennial kingdom, the rapture, the Book of Daniel, the Book of Revelation, and so forth. They were the most forceful interpreters of the typology to be found in the Old Testament. C. H. Mackintosh's *Notes on the Pentateuch* is considered to be a classic in this area of Biblical inquiry. In fact, the great evangelist Dwight L. Moody highly recommended it. They also clearly distinguished the prophecies in the Scriptures concerning the Jews and those concerning the Church — a great contribution in their day; for it must be noted that a hundred years ago many people tended to mix up these prophecies and thought that all these prophetic words to the Jews were fulfilled in the Church. Yet these Brethren produced many other writings as well.

During this same period, moreover, many spiritual brethren were raised up by God in England. Besides the few just now mentioned above, there were in addition such men of God as Charles Stanley and George Cutting. Cutting was the author of the widely circulated booklet entitled "Safety, Certainty and Enjoyment" which tells people that they may know they are saved. Hence the truth of the gospel had its well-rounded recovery by means of these brethren.

There was also Robert Govett who saw the truth concerning the Believer's Reward. He re-discovered the fact that although people are indeed saved through faith, each believer will receive a reward from God according to his works. Govett saw that to be saved is a matter of life; to be rewarded, on the other hand, is a matter of living. Charles Spurgeon once said that Robert Govett was a century ahead of his time because what he preached was too deep. This same Govett was the one who shared two more insights into God's truth: (1) that it is possible for Christians to be excluded from the millennial kingdom, it therefore requiring of believers to be faithful and diligent; and (2) that not all believers will be raptured before the Great Tribulation, meaning that only the overcoming and faithful ones will participate in the kingdom.

Another spiritual brother of some fame was G. H. Pember who wrote a number of books on prophecy. D. M. Panton, Hudson Taylor and many others left us their spiritual writings too. Taylor's *Union and Communion* revealed a deep experience of Christ. All these people made wonderful re-discoveries and recovered various truths, yet even theirs could not be reckoned as God's central truth. That would have to come later.

In England there was George Müller who was raised up by God for a specific testimony. He learned well in the area of prayer and faith. Müller testified that man could claim God's promises through prayer, and he also demonstrated a life of faith in financial matters.

On the North American continent, the Christian and Missionary Alliance Church sprang up. The most notable leaders in that Church group were A. B. Simpson and A. J. Gordon. They exerted great spiritual influence upon many believers. They announced that Christians should return to the experience of living by faith as had been true in the Apostolic Age of the first century. Such a view was an astounding revelation at that time. Thank God, this truth is generally practiced today here in our midst.

Both Gordon and Simpson also re-discovered the truth of Divine Healing, and there began in their midst the experience of the healing of sicknesses. This news spread quickly, it being advertised by many people and attracting huge crowds. Yet what Simpson and his associates emphasized was not the healing of sickness, but rather the overcoming of physical weakness through resurrection life and a triumphing over sickness by knowing Christ as the Mighty Deliverer.

At about the same time another group of people was raised up. Those within this group focused their attention upon the inner life of the Christian. About sixty years ago* God apprehended a merchant of china-wares whose name was Pearsall Smith. He uncovered the truth that one is sanctified through consecration. This approach to the subject was quite different from that of Wesley. For the sanctification Smith advocated was to be obtained through consecration by faith where-as the sanctification that Wesley preached was that a perfect life was gradually attained after consecration. Actually, both are true.

Along this same line of the inner life emphasis, there was Mrs. Hannah Whitall Smith (Pearsall Smith's wife) who wrote the classic work entitled *The Christian's Secret of a Happy Life.* There were also Evan Hopkins, Andrew Murray and others who in their lives and writings were the successors, as it were, to the teaching of self-denial as propagated two hundred years earlier by Madame Guyon and others. They began to hold conventions annually in Germany, England and other places. These convocations were the early beginnings of today's famed Keswick Convention. Frequently, one of the principal speakers at this kind of convention was Evan Hopkins. He received help from the two Smiths (Pearsall and Hannah) as well as from Madame Guyon. He exerted a definite positive influence on the contemporary spiritual world of his day.

---

*Dating back, of course, from 1934, it therefore being in the late nineteenth century.—*Translator*

Charles Trumbull is another instrument of God who should be mentioned. He it was who at the Keswick Conventions of his day had released the truth of the Victorious Life, thus contributing greatly to the recovery of the knowledge and experience of victorious living.

After Evan Hopkins there arose a sister of spiritual stature by the name of Mrs. Jessie Penn-Lewis. In her early years she was physically very weak and was often sick in bed. During her illness she read the writings of Madame Guyon, which writings she treated as her "pillow." At first Mrs. Penn-Lewis could not believe that total self-denial, full faith and perfect love as given in these treatises of Madame Guyon were practicable. One day she had a controversy with God, during which she earnestly asked the Lord to cause her to enter into these truths that had been released by Madame Guyon two centuries earlier. The Lord heard her prayer, and from that day onwards Mrs. Penn-Lewis was raised up by God to proclaim the truth of the cross.

Brother Holden of the China Inland Mission came to know the Calvary experience by reading the writings of Mrs. Penn-Lewis. She was truly one who bore the cross. The truth of the cross as lived out in her own personal experience greatly attracted people to seek after it. Through her writings God caused many to know that the cross is the centrality to God's work as well as the foundation of all spiritual things. As Mrs. Penn-Lewis saw it, without the work of the cross, man cannot and will not truly know what is death or what is sin. Many spiritual believers received much help from Mrs. Penn-Lewis and many experienced deliverance through the messages that God used her to give.

We have thus seen — in this all-too-brief survey of the third period in our discussion of Church history — that the re-discovery of God's truths was progressing quite rapidly and much more fully than in the two previous periods. In fact, it could rightly be said that by the end of the nineteenth century almost all the major truths had gradually been recovered.

Let us now look at the fourth and final period — the twentieth century. At very near the beginning of the present century there occurred a major event in modern Church history. Here I have reference to the great Welsh Revival of 1904–05 during which the entire population in some places was saved. But added to the widespread proclamation of the gospel, there also appeared many external manifestations reflective of the first Christian Pentecost.

The leader of this Revival was Evan Roberts, a twenty-six-year-old miner, with little education. Yet God called him among the humble and gave him a helper named Hastwell. After Roberts was saved he frequently prayed with great earnestness in the mine. His prayer was but one: "Lord, bend the Church to save the world." The people around him were moved in amazement. Gradually, many joined him in prayer. Soon, the laborers in the entire mine were affected and all gathered to pray. Revival thus broke out and spread over the southern part of the British Isles. From the Welsh revivalists we learn two important truths:

First, that the revival work of the Holy Spirit is invariably brought in by a group of bended and broken people. We have no need to ask God to pour out revival upon us; we need only to ask Him to bend and break us more. And as a consequence, life will spontaneously flow out from us.

Second, here was the beginning of the knowledge concerning the works of the evil spirits. Before that time some might have talked about this subject, but they lacked a thorough knowledge of it. Evan Roberts knew what spiritual warfare is. He alone in his day had a deep understanding of the experience of Ephesians 6. In 1908 while sick in bed, he related his experience on spiritual warfare and evil spirits to Mr. and Mrs. Penn-Lewis. Later on Mrs. Penn-Lewis combined these insights of Evan Roberts with her own experience to write a book entitled *War on the Saints* which set many deceived believers free. Indeed, within the past few years, the message which has occupied the most attention of spiritual believers has been mainly that of Mrs. Penn-Lewis, which is the truth concerning Spiritual Warfare and the Cross.

Simultaneously with this Welsh Revival, a new work of God began in Los Angeles, California, in the United States. In 1906 on Azusa Street in Los Angeles, gathered believers from among the black race experienced the outpouring of the Holy Spirit and began to speak in tongues. Since then, this practice in our own day seems to have become excessive and improper in its expression among many people. We do not deny the place of speaking in tongues and we, too, help people to experience Pentecost. The teaching of Paul, on the one hand, is: "Do all speak with tongues?" (1 Cor. 12.30), and, on the other hand, is: "Forbid not to speak with tongues" (1 Cor. 14.39). The first instruction of Paul here is given to those who would over-emphasize tongues, and his second instruction here is aimed at those who would overlook it altogether. As a matter of fact, we should pay attention to both.

These Azusa Street people, and those who followed them, have pointed out that the Old Testament prophecy found in Joel 2 had not been completely fulfilled during the Apostolic Era but would be fulfilled totally in the days of "the latter rain." And this phrase, "latter rain," in its spiritual application has reference to the present time.

Having thus far reviewed the re-discoveries of various truths of God in the centuries past as well as in our own century, we would now inquire into what has been the work of God in China recently. What is God's present work here?

When first saved myself, I heard various doctrines preached by many foreign missionaries. Before 1920 people in China had hardly even heard the gospel message. It was after that year that messages on the new birth, salvation, justification and other aspects of the gospel began to be proclaimed. Before that time many had not known what salvation was. We now have in China about 150 different denominations. God has shown us the error of Church disunity and has enabled us to preach messages on God's salvation and so forth. He gradually revealed various truths such as the aforementioned ones of the victory of Christ, the resurrection life, the cross, the Holy Spirit, and many others. We ourselves came to see these truths one after another. And in various other places in China other people also slowly came into an understanding of them. Furthermore, in our conversations with foreign missionaries we soon discovered that these same truths which we had come to know in China were likewise being re-discovered and recovered throughout the West.

We know that God's truths are cumulative, and hence, all these recovered truths of His of which we have been speaking serve as today's foundation. What we currently see are the accumulated revelations of God. And as He has opened our eyes to see this fact, we realize that we ourselves are living today in the current of God's will, a current which proceeds from all the past works of God. In the light of this, let us briefly review our own recent history.

Commencing with 1926, we have been releasing messages on salvation, the church and the cross, all of which we continue bearing witness to. In 1927 we particularly began to stress the subjective work of the cross. We began to see that the cross has its resurrection aspect as well as its death aspect. Formerly we had preached resurrection as an article of our faith and not as our experience. Now, though, we proclaim resurrection as a life principle: it is no longer a mere doctrine, it has become a spiritual reality in our everyday experience. For example, Jesus' parable about the grain of wheat falling into the ground and dying so as to bear much fruit is to us today a principle of resurrection. Besides these considerations, later on, God showed us what the Body of Christ is and where its reality is to be found. We came to understand that even as the life of Christ is one, so the Church is one.

I personally received much help from Mrs. Penn-Lewis. Brother T. Austin-Sparks of England was greatly helped by her, too. Brother Sparks was formerly a Baptist minister in the southeast area of London. The Lord showed him the truths concerning the cross, resurrection, church life, and other things.

We cannot say that these various truths were unknown before, but we do say that they were not as clearly known as they are today. Nevertheless, before the year 1928, we had not touched on the centrality of God's purpose. But in February of that year I began to teach something about God's eternal purpose. During almost the entire period of that month we had our first Victory Conference, which was followed by the second Victory Conference, held during October 8–18, 1931. The messages given in both conferences had been related to the centrality of God's will.

Yet in spite of the above comprehension, it was not until 1934 that we truly understood that the centrality of God is Christ himself. Christ is both the centrality and universality of God. In fact, all the plans of God, we came to learn, center upon Christ. This is the truth which God had caused us to see in those days and which is also the very theme for this third Victory Conference now underway—that of God's overcomers.*

And it should not be overlooked, incidentally, that the Lord has given much revelation to brother Sparks concerning the truth of God's overcomers. His overcomers are simply a company of believers who represent the whole Church of God and stand as vanguard on the ground of death to self. Their relationship to

---

*See the footnote at the very beginning of this Chapter for information regarding the release at this Conference of messages on this subject.—*Translator*

the Church is similar to the relationship between Zion and Jerusalem. All the demands of God towards Jerusalem fall upon the head of Zion.* And the apprehending of Zion is the apprehending of Jerusalem. And when God lays hold of both Zion *and* Jerusalem, His heart is satisfied.

We thank God with a full heart for the great helps we have received from all brethren who have preceded us. Yet as Paul once declared: "neither did I receive it from man, nor was I taught it, but it came to me through revelation of Jesus Christ" (Gal. 1.12); and hence, we can say that although we have indeed been helped by these brethren, the revelations we have were not received from men. Yes, we have been helped by Luther, Zinzendorf, the Moravian Brethren, the Keswick messages, and so forth. But today we believe that God's goal and end is "Christ all in all." That veteran servant of God, Dr. F. B. Meyer, saw this too. He confessed that being some ninety years old, he could not improve upon this description of it. I personally believe that God has but one work today, which is summed up in the message of Colossians 1.18: that "in all things he [Christ] might have the preeminence." The death, resurrection and ascension of Christ is the foundation. Apart from Him there is no spiritual reality. And such, may I say it, is God's "present truth."

We come back, then, to the question that was originally posed at the beginning of our discussion today, which was: What are we doing here? We would answer

---

*Zion is one of the hills of Jerusalem, and much identified with the life of David.—*Translator*

people's inquiry with the words of John the Baptist—that we are a voice in the wilderness. Our work is to call God's children to return to the central will of God, which is none else than accepting Christ as the centrality of all things and His death, resurrection and ascension as the foundation of everything. This is in fact the message of Colossians chapters 1 and 3. And in keeping with that message, we recognize that the place of the Church in the New Testament is a lofty and spiritual one. I would repeat what has been said before, that we do indeed thank God for the many helps which the foreign missionaries have over the years given us; nevertheless, God has sovereignly caused us to see today that everything must be brought back to the central will of God. Our work today is to return to the ground of the Biblical Church.

So that all the truths of God start with the Church. Paul was first placed in the local church at Antioch before he was ever sent forth to do the apostolic work that God eventually commissioned him to do. Likewise, in our own preaching of God's truths, we, too, take the local church as the starting point for our labors. Such is our work, such is our testimony.

Let us be those who lay stress less on the fragmentary truths. Let us be those who try to help people see the supremacy of Christ in all areas of spiritual life. We are not here to disturb the Church; rather, we are here for the purpose of assisting people to go back to the first work of the apostles. We should be careful in all things, rejecting all which is of men, and pursuing all which is of God.

We thank the Lord for calling us to His glorious

will. We need to be humble, subjecting ourselves to God and denying the self. May we see clearly that our work today is not limited merely to saving people and helping them spiritually, as good and as vital as these works are. Our present aim, however, is most high and glorious. Thank God that He has shown us His "present truth." May He be gracious to us that we do not fall behind in this present truth. And may we be watchful lest the flesh infiltrate where it should not and self be enthroned. May God's will be accomplished in us all.

Finally, I would add a few concluding words. Today we have a responsibility in four areas: (1) to preach the gospel to sinners; (2) to recognize spiritual warfare against Satan; (3) to maintain the vision of the Church as we have seen it; and (4) to testify to the fact that Christ must have the preeminence in all things. Today this testimony can also be found in America, England, France, Spain, and even in Africa. But the number of such testimonies is not large and the outward appearance is rather poor. Hence, we should pray for all these places.

6 | A Reply to the Brethren Assembly in London*

(Explanatory Note from the Magazine Editor: Several
years ago, eight believers who traveled from England, the
United States and Australia visited us in China and re-
quested to break bread with us. Owing to their being the
Lord's, we at once received them just as we always welcome
other people coming from the various denominations.

---

*This letter of reply was publicly circulated in the issue of the *Cor-
respondence* magazine dated July 1935.

Now in order for the reader to better appreciate the text of this
Reply that appears below, it was thought helpful to provide a brief
summary of the historical background to the matter. During October to December of 1932, six brothers and two sisters from the
Exclusive Brethren group in various parts of the West visited the
assembly in Shanghai and elsewhere for fellowship. These eight
believers came from England, Australia and the United States. And
as a consequence of their lengthy visit, Watchman Nee was in-
vited in the spring of 1933 to visit them in Britain and the United
States. Mr. Nee accepted the invitation and traveled overseas. But
during his visit abroad he not only had fellowship with these
Brethren but also managed to have fellowship with Christians out-

Knowing that they belonged to the Exclusive Brethren, we declared that we received them as individual believers and not as representatives of their fellowship. Later on, they asked us to adopt the same exclusive attitude as theirs. We prayed carefully, asking God for clearer light and appropriate words with which to give answer. The following is our reply.* All who read this document will know what our present belief on fellowship is and how we cannot join ourselves with the Exclusive Brethren. It is our sincere hope that Christians everywhere will not conceive

---

side their particular circle. This action by brother Nee was deemed by these Exclusive Brethren as having compromised his fellowship with them.

The correspondence which subsequently emerged as a result of the affair continued thereafter over a long period of time. The last reply sent by the brothers representing the brethren who met on Hardoon Road and North Szechuan Road in Shanghai took the form of a lengthy letter dated 2 July 1935, the contents of which now appear in the pages to follow. In essence it was a plea for open fellowship among all the saints everywhere. This, however, was unacceptable to the position taken by these Exclusive Brethren. So that on 30 July of the same year "a meeting of assembly character" was convened in London, at which it was decided to break off fellowship with the brethren in China whom the eight had previously visited. A letter dated 31 August 1935 was accordingly sent to communicate their decision, thus bringing the correspondence on this matter to a close.

It should be added that this Reply is given here with the sole purpose of illustrating the truth concerning fellowship. It is not to be taken as an attack or criticism against any group of God's children. God has had His choicest people among the Exclusive Brethren, and the Church at large has received much help from them.—*Translator*

---

*Watchman Nee was one of the six signatories to this Reply and the one who contributed most in formulating it.—*Translator*

our fellowship to be one comprised of those who have left the sects, but that instead they may know from this document that what we strongly maintain is the fellowship in the Holy Spirit.

We have received your former letter inquiring about this matter of fellowship. We should have replied earlier, but due to the lack of clearest light from God, we have delayed our frank reply till now. For we dare not act hastily without respect to God's will. Naturally such delay necessitates your love and patience. If we have inconvenienced you due to our delayed answer, we feel regretful and ask your pardon. Furthermore, since February of last year our brother Watchman Nee has been stricken with heart trouble. He has recovered only recently. This is another reason for the delay.

We believe all who are taught of God have no confidence in themselves. The flesh is totally useless even in the matter of knowing the word of God. People may grasp a truth in their mind, yet they remain totally ignorant of that truth as knowing nothing. Only in the Holy Spirit, in life, may we understand spiritual things. We are prone to stand on the revelation and light of other people, thus turning ourselves back to the law. The New Testament age is a spiritual age, therefore people might and ought to be taught inwardly by God and understand the truth inwardly (see Heb. 8). Whatever comes from outside (including the mind) and at the same time does not penetrate deeper in has no spiritual value. It is no different than not knowing at all. This, however, does not mean that we are not willing to be taught by our brethren. Yet we deeply feel that unless the Holy Spirit quickens the truth in us, we can do nothing. We would further say that the reason for the deadness and feebleness of the saints today is largely due to their receiving and following the truth with their mind. This is none else but the law. In spite of the exactness of letter, it is absolutely not of the Holy Spirit.

For this reason, we can only wait on God and rely on His Holy Spirit, instead of trusting our own mind. With hearts of thanksgiving, we believe that by His grace He has given us light and utterance. We firmly believe that this light comes from Him, and of this we now therefore wish to share with you. We earnestly pray that this letter comes solely from Him without any mixture of human idea.

(1) God's original thought concerning the Church is that she might be the "residue of Christ" or "the fullness of Christ." According to 1 Corinthians 12.12, the Lord Jesus and the Church are "the Christ" (Darby). The personal Christ and the Church are joined together to be "the corporate Christ." The Church should manifest Christ in her life and testimony. She is to display His life, His victory and His glory. In God's original thought as well as in this age, every child of His in this true Church is to bear witness of His only begotten Son.

(2) Alas, however, the flesh always spoils the things of God. Even before the apostles had passed away, "the ruin of the Church" (externally speaking) had already set in. Though men's sin had been forgiven and they had become children of God, they nonetheless could not manifest Christ, neither could they testify to His life, victory and glory. Only a few could still satisfy

God's thought. The vast majority began well, but when they had controversy with God, their life and testimony suffered. Henceforth in the Church there appeared two classes of believers, the overcomers and the overcomed (see Rev. 2,3). The overcomers are not superior to normal Christians, but the overcomed are inferior to normal Christians. The overcomers are those who satisfy God's original thought.

(3) As regards the question of fellowship, this presented no problem to the Church during the Pentecost period. For during that time all the believers in the Church were saved sinners and were saints with a testimony (here we are not talking about exceptional cases). Today's difficulty, though, lies in the divorce of these two aspects. Although people are saved, many do not live in the Holy Spirit. Should we maintain absolute, open fellowship with all the children of God regardless of their conditions? or must we restrict our fellowship only to those among the overcomers? Are we to start a popular Christian movement? or should we answer the call to overcome and pursue diligently God's perfect will?

From the seven letters to the seven local churches in Asia Minor found in Revelation chapters 2 and 3, it is evident that the Lord is now calling for overcomers. Though He has not forsaken ordinary Christians, His eyes are nevertheless upon that company of overcomers who will fulfill His original thought.

In view of this, we who gather on the ground of the Church and meet as a local assembly should answer God's heart desire by being a vessel for "the testimony of Jesus." It is not enough simply to be a popular movement among the saved. An assembly ought to be a vessel that witnesses especially to Christ.

The overcomers of the Church are those who in the time of Church declension are able to take up the responsibility which the whole Church ought to bear but has failed to do. They stand before God just as the Church ought to stand. (Compare with the remnants of the former age.) A local assembly today ought to stand on the ground of the Church and possess the nature of this kind of overcomer.

(4) Does this mean that we should be separated from other children of God? that we should decide who among the believers may or may not have fellowship with us? that we should determine who is an overcomer? or that we should refuse to fellowship with those whom we consider not spiritual enough?

The Scriptures plainly show us that the basis of our receiving one another is "even as Christ also received you" (Rom. 15.7). The reason why we receive anyone is because "God hath received him" (Rom. 14.3). Hence the command of God to us is: "him that is weak in faith receive ye" (Rom. 14.1). This command is explicit, distinctive and irrevocable. It is a sin to refuse acceptance of him whom God has received, however weak or lacking in light he may be.

Nevertheless, this does not imply that the defeated [who are unrepentant] may have fellowship with God and with God's people. Not only the world, the flesh and sin may deprive the *Church* of its characteristics and hinder its fellowship, even a slight deviation from the will of God and from the leading of the Holy Spirit may cause the *believer* to lose contact with God. An overcomer must not only be correct in his external position but must also live in the Holy Spirit.

Who among any of us is really worthy to undertake this work of selection—this act of determining who is fit for fellowship? From what we learn in the Bible, our responsibility is to judge only on moral corruption (1 Cor. 5.10–13) or on heresy regarding the Person of Christ (2 John). Difference in interpretation of truth alone must not be the ground of division.

Thus we receive all whom God has received for the sake of Christ.

(5) We need to distinguish the "sin," be it moral or doctrinal, that would or would not hinder fellowship with God. We know for sure that sins such as fornication and not believing that Jesus came in the flesh would block fellowship. But sins such as "denominational connection" and apparent errors of interpretation on prophecy do not cut off fellowship with God. This fact you cannot deny: that many who have not yet departed from what you call "evil association" and who, moreover, differ with you in prophetic views have most intimate fellowship with the Lord, even more intimate than we have. This clearly indicates that the so-called "evil association" and "evil doctrine" are not the sins which hinder fellowship. This also proves that he who stands on the correct ground of the Church and truth may not himself necessarily possess a close contact with the Lord. There is one thing far more essential than external ground and mental acceptance of truth, and that is, to live in the Holy Spirit and give no ground to the flesh. This is of the greatest importance.

The fellowship of God's children is in the fellowship of God's Son. It is also in the fellowship of the Holy Spirit. Whoever lives in the Holy Spirit has fellowship. The flesh has absolutely no place in the Holy Spirit. (It is reasonably permissable in babyhood, but it is totally unacceptable for a believer to remain in baby-hood.) Actually the act of receiving or not does not really bring one into or exclude one from the fellowship of Christ. The fact of the matter is: if he is truly in fellowship he *is* in fellowship, or if he is not truly in fellowship he is therefore *not* in fellowship. Appearance is of little value here; reality alone counts. The Holy Spirit alone knows who is not rebellious to His author-ity, does not grieve Him, and who lives in Christ through Him. And hence, the Holy Spirit alone can decide who may or may not have fellowship. We are not qualified to make such a decision.

We firmly trust this is the will of the Lord. We read-ily acknowledge that we must not receive anyone with-out judging any manifest sin or heretical doctrine in the person, but as to who may truly have fellowship is up to the Holy Spirit and not up to us. That person must also examine himself, for he himself has the re-sponsibility to examine himself in regard to this mat-ter of fellowship. Please see 1 Corinthians 11.27–34.

On the authority of the word of God and the lead-ing of the Holy Spirit, we have decided that people would have to be received by us before they could fellowship with us (see Acts 9.26–28; Rom. 14.1–3; 15.7; 16.2; 2 Cor. 3.1, etc.). This, however, does not mean that all who might be received by us may have fellowship. For the person received needs to examine himself before the Lord as to whether he is in fact worthy to fellowship. We can only distinguish who is a child of God and who is a child of the world. But as to selecting among God's children, the Lord has not appointed us as judges.

(6) Consequently, in practice, we feel after one is received he should be told that so far as the local church is concerned we are satisfied, but that his own condition before God is something he himself needs to be responsible for by his examining his own self. For only those who have fellowship with the Lord are qualified to partake in the Lord's Table. At each meeting, this practice and responsibility should be clearly stated so that no one would think because he is not excommunicated he is fit for fellowship.

(7) We are doubtful about your current way of reception. We wonder if this is a practice truly handled by the Holy Spirit or is simply a method received by men? Your custom of receiving may have been a living reality at the beginning, but many years of habitual practice have reduced it to a routine. Our basic question on this is whether it is men who are conducting this matter or whether it is the Holy Spirit who is exercising His authority?

(8) Some may question the safety of receiving people on the basis of their being Christians alone and leaving the responsibility of the partaking of the loaf* entirely to themselves. Let us be reminded that Christian

---

*Partaking of the loaf: a term used to denote participation at the Lord's Table or Last Supper in the local church.—*Translator*

fellowship is too spiritual a matter to rely upon the protection of human hands. Furthermore, if we are truly spiritual and not mental in our approach, we shall see the sovereignty of the Holy Spirit manifested in power and authority. But if we have only mental, and not experiential, knowledge of the Holy Spirit, confusion will be the natural consequence.

Do we not rely on the guidance and leading of the Holy Spirit in meetings? We give Him boundless position in exercising His sovereignty to choose any vessel He prefers to use, without any human arrangement. Why, then, can we not also trust the Holy Spirit to keep the purity of fellowship at the Lord's Table by His constraining or restraining the saints in the breaking of bread? If we give ground to the Holy Spirit in exercising His sovereignty, we do not need any man-invented method of exclusive reception as a substitute.

At the same time, we think of the distribution of God's workmen. In view of the vast territory of China, some are tempted to stand above all the servants of God and direct their works. How good indeed this is from the human standpoint! For will there not thus be equal distribution without any place having too many or too few workers? Yet however much man may seek the will of God, the Holy Spirit is nonetheless the sole Executor of God's work and He needs no man as His agent.

We must exercise faith to trust in the sovereignty of the Holy Spirit rather than planning to centralize finance. People like to distribute evenly to God's servants, thus no one will receive too much or too little. But where, then, is the sovereignty of the Holy Spirit in all this? During the past ten years we have tried diligently to give the Holy Spirit full sovereignty in this matter. We let Him guide the local assemblies as well as individual saints according to His direction. What we see as a result is: "he that gathered much had nothing over; and he that gathered little had no lack" (2 Cor. 8.15). We ought to allow the Holy Spirit to have sovereignty over all things.

No matter how we seek to know His will, we can never be His substitute. We must let the Holy Spirit do whatever He wills. Let us be clear as to whether it is the Holy Spirit who is now exercising His authority or whether we ourselves are trying to guard this fellowship.

(9) The reason for the lack of life in the assemblies today lies just here: the human hand has substituted itself for the sovereignty of the Holy Spirit. This, however, was not so in the preceding century. Judging by what we have heard and read, the assemblies in the former days had more life and power. Nor was there present in those earlier days the way of receiving as is known today. For then the Holy Spirit was the sole guide in both works and fellowship. It was due to the failure of men (as in the case of the Bethesda Chapel, in Bristol*) that human hands began to control this matter of receiving.

---

*In 1848 the church at Bethesda Chapel, Bristol, received two brothers from the meeting in Plymouth after having examined them and found them free from the error attributed to John Newton. This was considered by some as a failure to judge evil on the premise that association with evil was evil. This controversy over the principle of receiving—whether it is based on individual fitness or on association—eventually split the Brethren Movement into "Exclusive" and "Open."—*Translator*

Church history shows us that almost all denominations have had their beginnings in revival. The Holy Spirit commences His work through the vessel He has chosen. During the initial stage, people respect the Spirit and let Him have full sway. Thus blessings flow as living waters. Yet in order to preserve such blessings and to maintain some special truths that were revealed, men invent many rules, systems and organizations instead of maintaining the authority of the Holy Spirit among God's children. As a consequence, at a certain point in time the work of the Holy Spirit comes to an end while system and organization continue on with increasing strength.

(10) We would now make our position crystal clear. We do not stand on an open ground which overlooks matters that might bring reproach to the Lord. No, we absolutely do not take that position. Nor do we stand on the exclusive ground which is according to man's thought and not according to the Holy Spirit. We stand instead on the *spiritual* exclusive ground which means that we want our fellowship to be wholly in the Holy Spirit without any mixture of the flesh. To enjoy such kind of fellowship as this, the flesh must be thoroughly dealt with by the cross of Christ. For the flesh has absolutely no place in this fellowship. It is not sufficent merely to terminate so-called "evil association." The total life of the flesh must be dealt with. The power of the cross must be experienced by all through the working of the Holy Spirit. Mental knowledge is of little use.

This, then, is our fellowship. Accordingly, we are as open as the early Church that received all Christians, yet we are as exclusive as the Holy Spirit in rejecting all that is of the flesh. Many whom you reckon as in your fellowship are actually not so. Possibly the number of such people far exceeds our expectation. How very sad this is! For many believers, though they have passed your test of strict receiving, do not live in the Holy Spirit. Yet they consider themselves in the fellowship and freely partake of the loaf because they have not manifested sins! We cannot but regard such a standard of fellowship as too low.

The danger of human selection lies in either extending fellowship to the undeserved or refusing fellowship to the deserved. Have not these things happened in your midst? Such difficulties will be avoided among us all if we allow the Holy Spirit to make the choice and willingly step aside ourselves by trusting wholly in Him.

(11) This perhaps will conflict with your concept of right and wrong. For according to your view you consider many of God's children to be "wrong," and therefore you will not receive them. Nevertheless we need to learn to respect the Holy Spirit in a meeting. If *He* will supply and encourage them, even *use* them, we should do likewise. If the *Holy Spirit* can forbear certain things, why can we not? In any case, the fact of the matter is that many of God's children who differ with your system and whom you judge as unfit for fellowship are walking with God and maintaining sweet fellowship with the Lord. Does not this clearly indicate to us that fellowship is based on spiritual life and cessation of all fleshly works?

Some may oppose this because of the lack of external uniformity. We should be reminded that the flesh cannot endure outward irregularity. For it delights in orderly appearance. Rigid uniformity (law) is a thing of the flesh. In the New Testament there are letter and law just as in the Old Testament. It is only when we live in spiritual reality and understand all truths in life and not in the mind that we will pay more attention to spiritual reality than to outward appearance.

(12) We recall how the apostle Paul allowed liberty in matters concerning days and food. In our own day we would probably consider these external differences as too weighty in their significance to be given any liberty. If we were to learn that some people in our assembly eat only vegetables and keep the Sabbath, how uncomfortable and anxious we would be. Yet Christian oneness and fellowship is such a deep reality that it cannot be touched by these outward things. Furthermore, the Scriptures do not plainly record that those who preached out of jealousy and strife were ever formally excommunicated (see Phil. 1). And in the case of the failure in responsibility of an assembly to put away the wicked one (1 Cor. 5.2), neither this man (the wicked one) nor that assembly received any formal dealing except that the apostle exercised the spiritual authority that was given to him (1 Cor. 5.4,5). Even with the antichrists, the pertinent Scripture says that they voluntarily "went out from us" (1 John 2.19); they were not being excommunicated. These cases would teach us that the Lord cares little about external regularity during the time of ruin.

Please recall how the ark had at one time remained in the houses of Abinadab and Obed-edom (2 Sam. 6). What God desires is the full testimony of Christ (the ark), not the ordinance of divine service in the tabernacle. During the revivals of Nehemiah and Ezra, God gave recognition to them in spite of there being many differences between their day and the former days. Moreover, in the earthly days of Christ, we witness a group of people who possessed external exactness; yet Christ deliberately set aside these outward matters in order to lay stress on the more important ones. We believe that in today's apostasy the Lord is leading His people to see the value of spiritual things more than the exactness of outward appearances.

The Pharisees of that earlier time were people who kept the law: "as touching the law, a Pharisee" (Phil. 3.5). In this connection, we would inquire as to what is the ground on which you meet? Do your brethren surpass the rest of Christians in spirituality, in zeal for Christ and in separation from the world, or do you merely stand on a better Church ground than the others? If the characteristic of our lives does not lie in spirituality but only in exactness, then our very best is merely equal in value to the earlier Pharisee movement. How pitiful it is that having received so much light we are not more single-minded in our serving the Lord than people with less light.

(13) We do not despise the least of God's commands. We have no intention of straining out the camel and swallowing the gnat. We grieve for those who neglect the "small things" (Zech. 4.10) due to the dullness of conscience. For both "small things" and great things are equally the commands of God. Nevertheless, we also firmly believe that the "weightier matters" (Matt. 23.23) deserve first attention.

Do you realize that you too incur the danger of losing the living waters of the initial blessing and being left with a meeting system just as has happened in the other movements? You too will become a sect if you make external exactness the basis of fellowship instead of maintaining fellowship in the Holy Spirit.

Once several brothers in talking about "the fellowship of the apostles" touched upon the matter of the orthodoxy of fellowship. One brother rightly declared that orthodoxy lies in the Holy Spirit. We all need to see that the orthodoxy of fellowship is decided not by seniority, nor by "scripturalness," but by the full sovereignty of the Holy Spirit.

In order to unify interpretations and practices, you tend to divide God's children. Even the most spiritual among them will be divided into separate groups. We ourselves have no intention to forsake outward things so long as they are witnesses to spiritual reality (and not mere rituals and ceremonies). With instruction and love people can be persuaded to accept these outward things, but they should never be excommunicated for not receiving or having them. Otherwise, we too will become a sect, and death — not life — will prevail in the assembly. Many Church splits can be traced to this very cause.

(14) We need to understand what is "the unity of the Spirit" (Eph. 4.3) before we can know experientially the fellowship of the Holy Spirit. In each and every believer there dwells the Holy Spirit. By adding the Holy Spirit indwelt in one believer to the Holy Spirit indwelt in another believer and so on, we have "the unity of the Spirit." This unity, as the Scriptures tell us, we must

diligently keep (Eph. 4.3). But the flesh in us differentiates us one from the other, creating among us "strife, jealousies, wraths, factions, divisions, parties" (Gal. 5.20). For us to be able to keep the unity of the Spirit it is necessary for us to know by experience how the flesh is dealt with by the cross. Oneness comes to us when we let the Holy Spirit be Lord in our midst and we all follow the leading of the Holy Spirit. We cannot keep that which we do not possess. Unless the fleshly life in all its aspects is dealt with, there is no way to practice the unity of the Spirit. It is futile merely to *talk* about keeping the unity of the Spirit. If we *live* in the unity of the Holy Spirit, we will enjoy fully His fellowship. In this particular matter, the root of all evils is that saints today do not know what the crucifying of the flesh is, and consequently they do not know the Holy Spirit. We ask God to grant this revelation to His saints so that the life of the flesh might be judged. May the Lord do a deeper work in us all that we truly know what the flesh is.

(15) Beloved, the fellowship of the Holy Spirit is too spiritual a matter for us to guard, because it is indeed beyond our ability. We can only keep our fellowship from wicked ones. The Holy Spirit alone is able to preserve His fellowship. The human hand is totally useless in this matter of keeping the fellowship of the Holy Spirit.

Unless the Holy Spirit reigns in our lives we shall not enjoy the light and smile of the glorious face of our Lord, no matter how careful we are in outward things. We readily consent to the fact that in a locality where the Holy Spirit does not rule, the moment man's hand withdraws, chaos begins. Hence the fellowship of the assembly must be very spiritual so as to discourage the fleshly. So long as the Holy Spirit is in authority, the fleshly dare not "partake."

Beloved, may we humbly suggest that you carefully and prayerfully consider what we have here laid before you. We believe this that we have written is of God. Are you willing—as though knowing nothing at all—to lay aside your former preconceived thoughts written by you, and at the same time to ask the Lord to reveal to you whether or not what we have said is right and according to His will? This is indeed most serious, for the Lord is coming soon. Now is the time for us to make this matter clear before the Lord as eternity draws near.

We thank you for all that you have done for us. May God bless you. We also thank you for your patience in this matter. Once again, we ask your pardon for the late reply if we have inconvenienced you in waiting so long.

Your brothers in the Lord,

Representing the brethren met in
Hardoon Road and North Szechuan Road, Shanghai

7 | Concerning Workers*

One—The Raising Up of Workers

The first matter we wish to inquire into today is how a worker is raised up. Principally we will consider two different situations. The first happens where there is a local assembly. Where this is the situation, any brother who has the burden to work abroad needs to have the consent of all the brethren with whom he meets as well as to bear his personal responsibility before God. This can be likened to a finger of the hand which cannot move individually but must move only with the whole human body. It needs the sanction of the entire body before it can move. Today we see Christ as the Head of the Church, with the Church therefore constituting

---

*A talk with co-workers given by the author on 3 January 1934 at Hardoon Road, Shanghai, China, immediately after the conclusion of the Third Victory Conference. For more about this Conference see the footnote at the beginning of Chapter 5 above.—*Translator*

His body. So wherever there *is* a local assembly, there is always the need of getting the consent of the brethren. Take, for example, the situation to be found in Acts 13. There we see an assembly of believers situated in Antioch, and so we find that the Holy Spirit sent forth Paul and Barnabas through the local church there.

But where no local assembly exists, the situation is quite different. If there is no local gathering of believers, then a person who desires to go forth to work must bear his own responsibility directly before the Lord because an expression of the Body of Christ is not manifested there. In Acts 11, before the church in Antioch was established, Paul and Barnabas are found bearing responsibility directly before God. But later on, after the local church was formed at Antioch, the Holy Spirit is seen sending out prophets and teachers through the local expression of the Body of Christ. For by that time the work of Paul and Barnabas was no longer only a matter before God, it must now also be a matter in the church. There at Antioch the disciples laid hands on them and sent them out. The laying on of hands is for the purpose of showing sympathy and expressing union. Through this laying on of hands in the local assembly at Antioch, all the brethren joined with Paul and Barnabas in their mission. In essence, therefore, the going forth of these two was the going forth of the body of believers there. Yet it must be understood that such laying on of hands at Antioch was something vastly different from the practice we find nowadays called ordination. The latter is a form of human traditions, and is totally foreign to the Scriptures.

The sending out of Paul and Barnabas was for the

sake of doing the work the Holy Spirit sent them to do. This was the first missionary work in history. In this sending forth, the Holy Spirit has absolute sovereignty. A local church cannot send out men on its own. The sending out of the local church is the acceding to the movement of the Holy Spirit and the executing of His order.

In Acts 15 we read about another excursion contemplated. In verse 40, however, we notice the separation of the footsteps between Paul and Barnabas. Paul had suggested the journey, but Barnabas had insisted on taking Mark whom Paul deemed to be inappropriate for the task. There thus had arisen a sharp contention. Whereupon Barnabas decided to take Mark with him, but Paul took Silas with him and went a different way. It should be noted, though, that it is recorded in verse 40 that "Paul ... [was] being commended by the brethren to the grace of the Lord." Here, then, lies the difference between these two men. Paul was sent forth by the church, but Barnabas was not. Paul was commended by the brethren to the grace of the Lord, whereas Barnabas was not. In this conflict, the local expression of the Body of Christ stood on Paul's side. And as a consequence, we shall find that after chapter 15 Barnabas is no longer mentioned in the Acts narrative, thus proving that the Holy Spirit recognizes and ratifies the sending of the local expression of the Body of Christ.

In the instance before us now under discussion, we must note that Mark was passive, for he was a young worker under training. Hence his responsibility was not as great as that of Barnabas. Later, however, Mark was restored by God, and was once again brought back to the work by Him. But what about Barnabas? He was gone from the scene and never returned to the work of God. The Book of Acts never mentioned him again thereafter. Now if any of you should be tempted to say, "If others can, why can't I? Since a certain brother has gone to a certain place, why can I not go away, too?", then beware that that other brother of whom you speak is sent out properly in the context of the local church, whereas your going out will be strictly on your own. The difference lies just there. You cannot argue that if God could use him He could use you too. For God could indeed use him because he is sent out in the local body of believers, but He cannot use you. Do not fancy that God cannot lay any of us aside. He most certainly can lay us aside just as He laid aside Barnabas. How very clear and plain is the record found in the Book of Acts. For after this incident, the Holy Spirit ceased to mention Barnabas in the narrative.

A worker may do a work individually, but his movement must be in the church. This was the case at Pentecost: "Peter, standing up with the eleven, lifted up his voice, and spake forth . . ." (Acts 2.14) The "standing up" here is plural in number in the original Greek, whereas the "lifted up his voice" is in the singular number. Though only one man spoke, the eleven stood behind in support. Let us therefore realize that we too need the support of our brethren when we work.

Here we must learn the lesson of obedience. Both those who send and those who are sent need to learn obedience. Only in the spirit of obedience can people recognize the voice of the Holy Spirit. The criterion of any work is not approval but obedience. It is not because you approve of a certain brother that you therefore send him out. Many a time we may not approve the idea of a particular brother but we have to let him go, for the question lies not in approval but in obedience. Only in the obedient can the Holy Spirit find His outlet.

Now as the worker is sent forth he becomes an apostle, for an apostle is merely a sent-out worker. Paul was an apostle. What is the difference between an elder and an apostle? According to the word of God, an elder is immobile whereas an apostle is mobile. An elder is for a specific locality, but an apostle is for the entire Body. Paul was never an elder; he was only an apostle. Peter and John, though, were both elders and apostles. When they were in Jerusalem, they were elders of the church there. Yet besides being elders in Jerusalem, they were also apostles sent abroad. Because they were elders, they had the authority of local supervision. On the other hand, the responsibility of an apostle is to do the work committed to him abroad—he does not have the responsibility of overseeing in his own locality. I trust we are all clear on this distinction. When we talk about eldership we have reference to a locality; when we talk about apostleship we have in mind the whole earth. Yet it is possible for one person to perform both these functions—that is to say, to bear the responsibility of the local oversight as well as to bear the responsibility of the work of a wider sphere. In my own case, for example, my work on the one hand is serving workers at various places and on the other hand bearing responsibility with the other responsible brothers locally in Shanghai.

Two—The Confirmation of Workers

Let us now see who the workers are. How do we confirm a worker?

First, workers must have spiritual gifts. Gifts are of various kinds. Preaching the gospel is one kind, to be a prophet is another, and to be a pastor or teacher is still another kind. Different gifts result in different operations. The gift of an evangelist is towards the outsiders; the gift of a teacher is to decide on doctrine; and the gift of a pastor is to shepherd people — nourishing the spiritual life of the believers, causing that life to grow, and helping to solve all kinds of personal problems.

The more a worker is equipped with the above-mentioned gifts the better. A worker must at least possess one gift.

How do we know if a person has any gift? If you have a gift, the brethren who meet with you should be able to bear witness to the fact and confirm it. For this reason, the confirmation of gift is with the local body, which is able to sense it out. Whether your gift is that of an evangelist or that of a teacher, the body will perceive it. Even if you are not fully occupied with the ministry of God's word, you still could possess the above-mentioned gifts and thus do the work accordingly. For these gifts must be possessed by the workers, though they are not exclusively theirs.

Many think that if they are unsuccessful in working at one place they could change to another place and succeed. The fact of the matter is that the problem does not rest on locality. If a person is unable to work in one place, he is equally unable to do so in another. The issue is whether the person has a particular gift. A person not gifted is without gift at any place.

Second, a worker though gifted is nonetheless unable to work if his life is poor. For work depends on not only gift but also grace. It requires sufficient grace more than adequate gift. Although the result of a work is much related to gift, even so, it has more direct connection with the worker himself. Engaging in the same type of work, people with different grace will produce very different results. For the grace upon a person determines the work he accomplishes. It does not mean that the one who is without grace cannot lead others to Christ; in fact, he may be quite effective in winning souls since he has the gift of preaching the gospel; but due to the lack of life in him, the more work he does the more destruction he brings in. Today many workers build on the one hand and demolish on the other. The explanation for this lies in the lack of life.

As recorded in Acts 16.2, the brethren reported well of Timothy; and hence we find in verse 3 that Paul took him in the journey. This is the witness of the brethren. Timothy is not only confirmed in one place, he is confirmed by the brethren belonging to two places. If your condition before the Lord is good and you have sufficient grace, the brethren who meet with you shall surely testify concerning you. And not only those who are spiritual, even the not-so-spiritual shall testify for you.

*Three—The Relationship and Position of a Worker
to the Local Assembly*

According to the Scriptures an assembly should have three kinds of people: (1) those who believe in the Lord are basic to an assembly. Each and every assembly must at least have this kind of people; (2) those who serve in physical things. Theirs is mainly the mundane works such as managing various affairs for the brothers and sisters, together with assisting in the managing of church affairs. This group of people is called "deacons" in the Bible, and include both male and female; and (3) there are several brothers whose work is to be responsible for all the major matters of the assembly such as leading the meeting, deciding on issues, caring for the brethren, and dealing with the outside. This group of people is called "elders" in the Bible.

All three kinds of people should be present in an assembly. Here we include no worker because he has no special position in the local church. Since a worker is not someone special in the assembly, he must belong to one of the three kinds of people just now mentioned. He does not form a fourth kind of person in the local church.

The relationship among these three kinds of people may be illustrated as follows: Suppose the brethren in a certain locality need to build a meeting place. At the beginning the elders would make the decision on the matter. Then they would notify the brethren and designate various responsibilities to the deacons, who in turn would invite brothers and sisters with related professions to proceed with the job. At the most, the worker might *contribute* his part to the project; he could never *control* the whole work. He differs from the other believers only in his being able to bear more of a load. Such is the relationship between the worker and the local church.

As regards the position of what we today call "workers," it is no different from that of the apostles in the early days. They indeed have the work of the apostles today, but they do not have the authority of the apostles. Nonetheless, if a worker receives a special burden or commission from God, the local church should show its sympathy and support the work. We cannot find in the Bible any instance in which the local assembly disapproved of the burden of the apostle or in which the local church controlled the work of the apostle. The work of God would suffer greatly if such were ever the case.

Four—The Relationship between the Older and the Younger Workers

What is the nature of the relationship between the older and younger workers? According to the Scriptures, the latecomers should submit to the early comers: "the younger be subject unto the elder" (1 Peter 5.5). It is quite evident that Paul led Silas, Timothy, Titus and others. The latter clearly accepted the leading of Paul and also submitted to him.

Today two types of situations are found in the denominations. One extreme is that a worker is totally controlled and bound by the people above him. All decisions are made by human will. The other extreme is that with the so-called free-lance evangelists, they move independently and alone, eating their own food and preaching their own gospel, and are under the control and restraint of no one. Neither of these two kinds of people really knows the way of the Lord. For the first kind puts sovereignty into the hands of men. They do not recognize the Lord. The second kind of people holds sovereignty in their own hands and likewise fail to acknowledge the Lord. To place full sovereignty into the hands of the Lord alone, we must break away from both extremes. A worker must not be controlled financially by man nor can he surrender the authority of the Lord to other people.

Acts 8 tells us that Peter and John were sent by the Jerusalem church to preach in Samaria. Their footsteps were constrained by the local church. A worker is one who is under restraint. Many misconstrue a spiritual man to be one without restraint.

As regards the fulfillment of young people, the Bible does not bear any evidence of having offered or promoted the establishment of a theological seminary. Although we find in the Old Testament that some did set up a school for prophets, the fact of the matter is that no recognizable prophet had ever been produced by that school. Studying theology does not make one a worker. The training of a worker comes by way of the path of following and of obedience.

Timothy and Silas followed Paul. The Scriptures provide us with a system of *apprenticeship,* not a system of scholarship. Unless a young worker learns well in the area of obedience he is not able to learn well in any other area. This is of tremendous importance. Before a young worker becomes useful he must be pressed under the hand of God. Each one who has ever been used of God has gone through strict discipline. This you can readily see, for example, in Paul's letters to Timothy. How very strict were Paul's instructions to this young worker. He was neither casual nor indulgent towards Timothy.

Five—The Preaching of Young Workers

Many a time today's problem of the church begins with people's desire for more gifts. They assume that they have a certain gift, whereas in actuality they may not possess that particular gift. And so they spoil the work in their hands. They mean well, but they have simply not been given that gift; and hence they are unable to accomplish it. It is just like one who may have the gift of a teacher but he cannot do other works: he can only fulfill his portion of work in deciding on the truth of the Scriptures or maintaining that truth or discovering new truth. As another example, a person with the gift of an evangelist can only do his work of evangelizing: he cannot be a substitute for the teacher in teaching or deciding on truth: he can only fulfill his own part.

The problem today lies in the fact that few if any in the whole world stand in their proper place and are satisfied with their own position. The evangelist wants to be a teacher, and the teacher desires to be an evangelist. Everyone admires being what he is not. What is this? Is it not the manifestation of the flesh, the inclination of the natural man? Yet in the Body of Christ each member has his distinct function. The ear cannot be a substitute for the eye, nor the eye the ear. Even should the ear be located on the eye, the ear still remains an ear, for it cannot see. Here we discern the necessity of standing firmly in one's own position. Each one of us must learn to stand in his own place.

Personally speaking, young workers need not only be subject to the older workers but also to know what is God's appointed place for them. By recognizing your given place you will not fall into the flesh, thus saving the work. Naturally, in the event that a young worker truly has the gift of teaching while the older workers around him lack that gift, then under such circumstances the older workers need to submit to the younger worker and accept his given gift. Nevertheless, each young worker should try to find someone more mature from whom he may learn obedience. There must be some older workers to whom he can be subject. Paul told Timothy to "abide thou in the things which thou hast learned and hast been assured of, knowing of whom thou hast learned them" (2 Tim. 3.14). Timothy needed to find out from whom he had learned. He had to go and find the worker who was ahead of him.

A young worker must learn to accept unreasonable dealings. He should understand what unreasonable submission is. For true submission does not argue: if there be reasoning, then obedience is gone. In the work of God, no one can be independent nor can he escape submission. The young need indeed to be submissive; but then, too, the older is not to be an exception either. We cannot afford to be independent. If God should reveal a new truth to a brother, that brother must go forward in the spirit of mutual submission. He must not take any independent action.

Six—The Faith of the Worker

All workers must have the same faith in the Person and work of Christ. We all need to maintain in our life and work these foundational truths. Should any worker commit error in these basic principles, the elders should stop him from working. Concerning certain cardinal truths, there ought to be proper scriptural interpretations which are commonly accepted. The accurate interpretations of many Biblical passages have already been discovered by others. We need only to receive from them, without our adding on to them. There is a basic principle in studying the Scriptures—which is, to accept God's spoken word in simplicity, without adding on our own idea. As we study the word of God we need to ask of ourselves, "What has God spoken?" and not, "Why does God so speak?" It is not unlike the situation wherein a citizen of a country has no need to ask why there is a certain law—he merely inquires as to what the national law is. We should therefore ask "what" and not "why." For our basic attitude towards God's command should not be preeminently a matter of understanding but a matter of obedience.

Due to our different walks before God, different interpretations of the Scriptures arise. Take baptism as an example: Many who were baptized by sprinkling see the teaching of sprinkling in their Bible study. Such teaching is the product of their walk. A person's attitude before God has much to do with his interpretation of God's word. Many come to His word with the hope of finding out some rule which will justify his own walk. Their motive is to transform the word of God to be a law which suits them. And hence, they interpret the Bible for themselves. One who has not been dealt with by the cross is unable to study the Scriptures. He who has gone through the cross may alone read the Bible correctly.

Seven—The Needs of the Workers

Before we look at the needs of the workers, let us mention first this matter of offerings. A Christian's offering is not just for the sake of supporting workers as individual believers but is for the reason of supplying the needs of those who work for the Lord. In other words, it is not because a certain person is a worker that he is therefore being supported. He is supported because *he serves the Lord.* He as an individual person is one thing, and he who is in the work is another. So long as he works for the Lord, he deserves to be supported. The issue lies not in whether or not he is financially well, but rather whether he is working for the Lord. He who works for the Lord is worthy to be supported. It is similar to the matter of paying a rickshaw coolie, wherein we would never ask whether he is poor or rich. His poverty or abundance has nothing to do with it. It is simply that for his labor he must quite naturally receive his wages. Nobody can say that because a certain worker has money he therefore need not be supported. Not so. Once there was someone who was thinking of giving an offering to brother Bright, a co-worker of Dr. Scofield; but then he heard a person beside him say that the Lord could supply brother Bright's need. With the result that he withdrew his offering and left brother Bright in want. Let us see that the offering of a believer is not decided on the basis of the poverty of the worker. If support is given on the basis of poverty, such support is not an offering but is an expression of alms giving.

To present an offering is the least a person who has received grace must do. Without this, he is useless before God. His having received grace ought to produce the result of offering up all he has to the Lord. It is quite irregular for the one who has received grace to withhold offering. This is because as one's heart is touched by God that one's purse will decidedly be offered up. How can a person's heart be touched by God and yet his possessions not be touched? Offering is the clear evidence that our all has been touched by God, and thus there will be love flowing out from us. A person who fails to offer has no outflow of love.

In this world today there are only two gods: the one is Mammon (riches, wealth, possessions, etc.), and the other is the true God. If we do not love God, we must love Mammon. But when we love God, our heart is expanded and we just give. We have a believer in our midst who for twenty years met in a certain church without ever greeting anybody. But then he commenced giving an offering, and immediately his entire being was transformed. Formerly I dared not speak or report on the matter of offerings, but now I have turned myself around on this issue because I realize that this matter of offering up of our substance is a way to receive more grace. The more a person offers up, the more fully he receives of God's grace. And what I have said here today to you workers I say to all local churches.

Now let us see how offerings ought to be managed locally. Out of the offerings received by the assembly, a portion should be taken to support workers—both those locally and those abroad. This is for the purpose of expressing fellowship. In Philippians 4 we read how Paul commended the grace the Philippian believers had exhibited in their conduct. For they had continuously had fellowship with the apostle in their financial gift-giving. The situation of the Corinthian believers, though, was just the opposite. Because a problem existed between them and Paul in fellowship, Paul would rather do what he felt compelled to write in 2 Corinthians 11.8 ("I robbed other churches, taking wages of them") rather than be a burden to the Corinthian believers. And why? Because fellowship between them was a problem. But where there is fellowship—as in the case of Paul with the Philippians—there is offering.

Thank God, the brethren in Shanghai have received grace in this matter. You workers abroad, please do not misconstrue that the assembly here is so rich that it always sends out gifts. The reason why it is able to send out gifts is because the workers in Shanghai receive less local support. This constitutes the grace of the assembly here.

In giving personal gifts, it is best if the offerer would

first wrap up the offering, put the name of the worker on it, and then cast it into the offering box. The brothers who open the offering box can personally hand over the gift to the designated recipient.

Eight—The Way a Worker Manages Finance

(1) A worker should not let people know that he is poor. For a worker lives by faith, not by philanthrophy. It is a shameful thing to let people know about his poverty in order to receive supply. A worker must possess a proper attitude in receiving supplies. He represents God in receiving offerings from a brother. He stands on God's side, and therefore he must not give people a deplorable feeling. When Paul mentioned this matter of finance, the impression he gave was honorable and decent. Such is the right attitude each and every worker must have.

(2) Among the workers themselves, whenever there is a surplus in supply, it needs to be distributed. Do not by this action be afraid of being misunderstood as rich and wealthy. Then, too, for your personal family livelihood, some short-term savings is a principle agreeable to the word of God. The Book of Proverbs contains such teaching and exhorts us to do so.

(3) The spending of money should be planned. Many tend to buy unnecessary things when they have excess funds. Such behavior will hinder God's giving. The use of money should be planned according to a budget. The things to be purchased need to be well con-

sidered before God. Do not buy carelessly, and do not spend wastefully.

(4) A worker must not fall into debt. A servant of God would rather die than ask for money. If he does not have the faith for his livelihood, then he should seek some other "employment" by which to support himself. If he has faith in God to sustain his living, he will not stretch forth his hand towards man.

Nine—The Principle of Manna

Today Gods wants us to live according to the manna principle, which is this: "he that gathered much had nothing over, and he that gathered little had no lack" (Ex. 16.18). This is not just the record of the Old Testament. The New Testament, too, teaches this principle (2 Cor. 8.15). Much or little is equally wrong. If in an assembly some brothers have no means to maintain their living, either the church there or some individuals should help them. The local church cannot look upon the plight of unemployed brethren without its helping them the best way it can. This does not, of course, include those who refuse to work. People who are unwilling to work should not be helped; only those who are willing to work ought to be assisted. Furthermore, to those brothers who work but earn less than is sufficient for their livelihood, the local church must also render help. In the early Church, this principle was observed by the apostles.

As regards the order of rendering help and assistance, the local assembly must first take care of the brothers and sisters within the local church, and then help the poor outside. If a believer has near relatives who need help, he should help them first before he helps other people.

Do not offer aid casually without careful consideration. A person who is naturally "hand loose" in his giving is not blessed because he gives more. For he who would be "hand loose" is also carelessly loose in other things of God. We need to learn to be responsible offerers and not "hand loosers."

A believer's offering of assistance does not end with his giving out funds. He must in addition live a proper life before God so that his giving will be blessed. Thank God, not all are Lazarus, and not all are the rich man. What God wants is neither a Lazarus nor a rich man, but the offerings of those who live worthily before Him. The flesh commits either one of two sins before the Lord — either exercising "severity to the body" as Paul spoke of in Colossians 2.23, or else exercising over-indulgence to the body. What God ordains is neither severity nor indulgence to the body but the living of a godly life before Him. Any surplus funds should be freely distributed.

Ten — Concerning Letters of Recommendation

Finally, let us touch briefly concerning the letter of recommendation. Paul mentioned this matter to the Corinthian believers (see 2 Cor. 3.1). So we see that the New Testament does indeed deal with this subject. When believers travel to new places they have the need of letters of recommendation. Paul in his Epistle reminded the Corinthian believers that he had no need of such a letter. This was because he had a relationship with them. So that he is an exception. But for ordinary believers such a letter is essential. For it serves two purposes: (1) in causing you to be known; and (2) in preventing false brethren from coming in. Every letter of recommendation should be signed by three persons to assure its authenticity. Ordinary letters of recommendation are best written by the local elders or responsible brothers. There are at least three different kinds of letters:

(1) To recommend a certain person to partake in the breaking of bread, confirming him to be a brother or sister in the Lord.

(2) To recommend a certain person as one who walks in the same straight path.

(3) To recommend a certain person as not only walking in the same acceptable path but as also having a particular gift, thus providing an opening for ministry.

Upon receipt of a letter of recommendation, the local responsible brothers should acknowledge such letter by writing to the place where the letter originated. For the sake of convenience, such letters of recommendation and their appropriate reply could be prepared and printed beforehand for ready use. When brethren come from abroad or go abroad, let such letters of recommendation be given so as to facilitate the receiving of such at the table of the Lord.

8 | The Tempter and the Tempted*

One—The Origin and Kingdom of the Tempter

The Tempter is a created being who was fashioned with beauty and wisdom, perfect and powerful. Due to his desire to be equal with God, he sinned and fell: "thou saidst in thy heart, *I* ... " (Is. 14.12–14). Having lifted up his "I," he was cast out of the paradise of God, and the Scriptures tell us of his ultimate destiny: "yet thou shalt be brought down to Sheol, to the uttermost parts of the pit" (v. 15). Some of his followers were "cast ... down to hell, and committed ... to pits of darkness" (2 Peter 2.4). Since this Tempter fell through the sin of aspiring to be equal with God, he tempts people with the same ambition of being equal with God— which serves as his bait (Gen. 3.5–7). Let us therefore be watchful "lest being puffed up [we] fall into the con-

---

*This article was prepared by the author and published in *Spiritual Guide* in 1927.—*Translator*

demnation of the *devil*" (1 Tim. 3.6). We Christians ought to take Christ as our personality, which means we exercise our will to join with Christ. If we still let the old man be "I," we will be divided from Christ. The more we are in Christ the more we must understand things about the Tempter. And hence, the reason for this study.

1. His names. According to Revelation 12.9, he has four different names: The *Great Dragon* indicates his *cruelty;* the *Old Serpent* discloses his *deception*; the *Devil* speaks of his *temptation;* and *Satan* tells of his *hatred.* "The god of this world" in 2 Corinthians 4.4 refers to his being the head of the religions of the world. "The prince of the world" in John 14.30 alludes to his being the chief of world politics. "The prince of the powers of the air" in Ephesians 2.2 adverts to his being the king of evil powers. Revelation 12.10 says he is "the accuser of our brethren," and 9.11 states he is "the angel of the abyss." To the unwatchful and careless he is "as a roaring lion" (1 Peter 5.8). And to the watchful believers, he "fashioneth himself into an angel of light" (2 Cor. 11.13–15).

2. His kingdom. "The whole world lieth in the evil one" (1 John 5.19). This confirms that the Devil was not speaking empty words when he declared to Jesus while tempting Him, "To thee will I give all this authority ["all the kingdoms of the world"—v.5], and the glory of them: for it hath been delivered unto me" (Luke 4.6). By reading Luke 11.14–18, 20–24, we know that *men* are also included in the scope of the Devil's kingdom.

3. His government and subordinates. By reading Revelation 2.13 we know where the Tempter's dwelling place is. From reading Ephesians 6.12 we know all those who are in his army. Through reading Daniel 10.13,20 we learn about his subordinates. And as we read 2 Corinthians 12.7 we know something about his messengers.

4. His religion. Satan also has his religion, a worshipping with the spirit of confusion: "the blasphemy of them that say they are Jews, and they are not, but are a synagogue of Satan" (Rev. 2.9). This indicates that the words spoken in the synagogue of Satan are but words of blasphemy and of distortion! How many are the synagogues of Satan today! Full of criticism and doubt, mocking and slandering — this is the religion of Satan. 1 Corinthians 10.20–21 mentions about "sacrifice to demons" and "the cup of demons," thus revealing that Satanic religion also has sacrifice and communion. 1 Timothy 4.1–4 speaks of the "doctrines of demons." By studying carefully these four verses we come to know how the present-day apostasy concurs with the Scriptures. We thereby also discern that this present time is really the end time. How very pitiful that those who believe in the doctrines of demons do not realize they are of the demons. They not only follow but also propagate them.

5. His people. (a) *Satan works in the hearts of men without their knowing it:* "according to the prince of the powers of the air, of the spirit that now worketh in the sons of disobedience" (Eph. 2.2). (b) *Satan blinds the eyes of men:* "the god of this world hath blinded the minds of the unbelieving" (2 Cor. 4.4). (c) *Satan gives false peace:* "When the strong man fully armed guardeth his own court, his goods are in peace" (Luke 11.21). Those who are under the power of Satan think they have great peace, not realizing that such peace is unreal and is available only when everything goes smoothly. It is not the true peace and blessing which the Christians have. (d) *Satan secretly stirs people to oppose the truth:* "in meekness correcting them that oppose themselves; if peradventure God may give them repentance unto the knowledge of the truth, and they may recover themselves out of the snare of the devil, having been taken captive by him unto his will" (2 Tim. 2.25–26). Many are those who rebel and oppose the truth today. Actually, they have been taken captive by the Devil and have fallen into his snare.

Two—The Tempter and Those Who Overcome Him

1. The Overcomer. Besides our Lord Jesus Christ, there is no other: "To this end was the Son of God manifested, that he might destroy the works of the devil" (1 John 3.8); "he [the seed of the woman] shall bruise thy [the serpent's] head" (Gen. 3.15). Christ is the Overcomer who destroys the works of the Devil and breaks his head. Christ has overcome. By constantly confessing this fact and joining oneself to Christ, one may always triumph. What Satan fears most is "the word of their testimony" in the mouth of the saints to the effect that Christ is the Victor (Rev. 12.11). Such a word of testimony will cause him to flee. Christ is Victor! Hallelujah, praise the Lord! (see Mark 1.24,27; 3.11).

2. The place of victory. Apart from Calvary, where else could the place of victory over Satan be? The cross of Calvary is where Satan and his powers are defeated. The victory of Calvary is still powerful today: ". . . nailing it to the cross; having despoiled the principalities and the powers, he made a show of them openly, triumphing over them in it" (Col. 2.14–15); "that through death he might bring to nought him that had the power of death, that is, the devil" (Heb. 2.14). Many think that Christ crucified was the Lord's defeat, not realizing that this is where the victory was won. At the end of this age two armies will confront each other. But the battle is won without fighting. For when Christ was crucified and raised from the dead, He had entered into death, fought with it, and conquered it. The victory was then and there secured. His victory over Satan was not accomplished without His death and resurrection. In death Christ fought with Satan — who had the power of death — and conquered him. His resurrection is the evidence of His victory. As He moved forward, with His face towards Calvary, He declared: "Now is the judgment of this world: now shall the prince of this world be cast out" (John 12.31). Satan was defeated at the cross. Waging war against Satan in any other place would have ended in defeat. Satan is victorious in all places except Calvary. He was defeated *only* at the cross, and he was forever defeated there. So that all who are joined to the Lamb of Calvary stand on the ground of the victory of Calvary. They are not opening a new frontier; rather, they are applying that former victory to this present conflict. And in so doing, they shall overcome. Defeat is due to our depending upon self, but victory is because of standing on Calvary. The cross is the victory ground! Calvary is our home! What, then, do we have to fear?

3. The battle announced by messengers. We are the Lord's messengers. We proclaim the victory of Calvary and Christ the Victor: "I send thee to open their eyes, that they may turn from darkness to light and from the power of Satan unto God" (Acts 26.17–18). The victory of Calvary is still in effect today. Jesus the Savior is still the Conqueror. And Satan is still the vanquished. Satan has no power over us, for we have been delivered from the power of Satan unto God.

4. The captives freed. ". . . who delivered us out of the power of darkness, and translated us into the kingdom of the Son of his love" (Col. 1.13). Christ has overcome, and He is now overcoming. We are at this present moment in His kingdom, for we have been translated out of the power of darkness. Let us keep this fact well in mind, and trust in Him; and thus the power of darkness shall never come upon us. Always declare this position with faith and will. This is the best way to keep ourselves in that position.

5. The victory of the Christians. Christ is the Over-comer. We are in Christ; and being united with Him, we too are overcomers. We may overcome every day, for our Lord says to us: "Behold, I have given you authority to tread upon serpents and scorpions, and over all the power of the enemy: . . . the spirits are subject unto you" (Luke 10.19,20); "in my name shall they cast out demons" (Mark 16.17; see also Acts 16.18; 19.15). Outside of Christ we can do nothing. We need to abide in Him and do all things in His name. Satan then will always be defeated.

Three—The Wiles of the Tempter

Though Satan is most wileful, "we are not ignorant of his devices" (2 Cor. 2.11). What, then, will be the use of his trickery? Unfortunately, though we know his cunning, we are often not watchful. In Christ we should discern all things through depending on the Holy Spirit. If so, we shall be able to detect all the maneuvers of Satan, and by the Lord's power we shall make them ineffective.

1. His artifice against the unsaved. A certain class of unsaved people love to hear the word of God, but Satan steals the word away. It is written in the Scriptures: "those by the way side are they that have heard; then cometh the devil, and taketh away the word from their heart, that they may not believe and be saved" (Luke 8.12). What the Devil is afraid of is God's word, not a dissertation on the word. In our preaching let us be careful not to speak carelessly lest we lose the power of God. Whenever the Devil sees the word of God he will try to take it away. The minds of the unsaved, the uninterested, and of even those who are on the verge of believing have been blinded by the Devil: "in whom the god of this world hath blinded the minds of the unbelieving, that the light of the gospel of the glory of Christ, who is the image of God, should not dawn upon them" (2 Cor. 4.4). We ought to pray that the minds of the unsaved would be opened to receive the word of the Lord, and that it might grow and bear fruit.

2. His stratagem against the saved. (a) He causes them to have incomplete consecration (Acts 5.3). God is a jealous God. He demands full consecration, loving Him with all our hearts, all our minds, all our strength and all our soul. He wants us to be so selfless that we would not retain any part of our offering for self-consumption. Satan, however, is most afraid of our *total* consecration, for in so doing he will lose his working field. "Why hath Satan filled thy heart ... to keep back part of the price of the land?" (Acts 5.3) Satan had filled the hearts of this couple (Ananias and Sapphira) in that they kept back a part for their own use and yet claimed publicly they had offered all. How many are the believers today who know they should offer, and yet they consider the price too high; so they cheat themselves as well as others by keeping back a part for themselves and offering the rest to God in pretence of a total offering. Do they know how Satan has filled their hearts? Let each reader ask himself if he has fully consecrated.

(b) He hinders them from taking off the filthy garments (Zech. 3.1–3). When in Jesus' famous parable the prodigal son comes home, his father puts the best robe on him. The son will never wear his beggarly clothes in his father's house. Clothes represent righteousness. Satan is afraid of man removing his old righteousness. So he frequently entices man to establish a righteousness other than the righteousness of God (see Rom. 10.3). We ought to put on the Lord Jesus as our righteousness and get rid of that self-made righteousness of service and sacrifice as advocated by today's moralists. "Satan standing at his [the high priest Joshua's] right hand to be his adversary.... Now Joshua was clothed with filthy garments" (Zech. 3.1,3). Satan would not have us taking off that which naturally

belongs to us. Although believers have already been saved by trusting in the Lord Jesus as their righteousness, they are often deceived into retaining all their natural righteousness. Their old garments were naturally filthy, yet these are still their garments. Their own righteousnesses were filthy, but still are recognized as righteousness. So that Satan causes them to do good in their own power, stirring up their original righteous deeds in order to please God and obtain men's praise. Do they not know that their old garments are as filthy rags before God? Our natural righteousnesses are totally unacceptable to Him. Nonetheless, Satan wants us to use our soul power to execute the will of the spirit. Let us therefore be very careful.

(c) He drives believers to work with fleshly envy and strife (James 3.14–15). Satan is not willing to see Christians being united in one. If he finds two believers in agreement, he will try to split them apart. If he discovers three disciples in unity, he will break up their harmony. If he learns of more being together, he will smash their oneness. He will sow jealousy and strife in the hearts of the believers so that they will refuse to work together. This happens in spiritual works as well as in secular works. Believers are deceived into musings like this: "You are stronger spiritually than I am; you are more appreciated in preaching than I am; your interpretation of doctrine is different from mine." All these create envy and strife. How poisonous are such strifes in the hearts of men. And how dangerous they are, for they are not easily detected in appearance.

(d) He hinders believers from the cross by means of other people: "Peter took him, and began to rebuke

him, saying, Be it far from thee, Lord: this shall never
be unto thee. But he turned, and said unto Peter, Get
thee behind me, Satan" (Matt. 16.22–23). The defeat
of Satan is at the cross, therefore he is most fearful of
people going to the cross and obtaining the victory of
Calvary. Here he was bold enough to tempt the Lord
Jesus, enticing the Latter to mind the things of men
instead of His minding those of God. The Devil is skill-
ful in manipulating human affection, causing people
to depart from the way of the cross by judging it to
be too difficult, too painful. To walk in it indicates a
lack of self-preservation. But to mind the things of men
automatically shuts off the minding of the things of
God. Irrespective of self-pity or considering others,
God's will shall suffer. When "I" is in ascendancy, Satan
can easily put what is his into it. Self-love, self-esteem,
self-pity—these all travel in the opposite direction from
the cross. Human consideration, sympathy, fear and
compromise—these, too, run opposite to Calvary. In-
ability to deny self and human affection is the method
Satan uses to stop men from going to the cross. Satan
trembles at seeing people crucified and resurrected (see
Matt. 16.21). Consequently, he tries his best to block
them from the cross. But the Lord has appointed for
us no other way except the cross (1 Thess. 3.3). What
way are you taking today? How very sad that nowadays
many Christians see the cross and by-pass it because
they are not willing to be crucified. The affliction may
be avoided and self may enjoy peace, but the will of
God is missed. With real death, there comes real resurrection. There, Satan has no foothold. This he hates
most. Since Satan is afraid of our going to the cross

and dying and being resurrected, we must all the more die to self and be resurrected from the dead by faith in the Lord.

(e) He threatens as a roaring lion (1 Peter 5.8). Satan not only entices in secret, he even dares to seek the careless and unwatchful to devour. Satan threatened Martin Luther with a scroll on which was written all of his sins, tempting him to doubt his salvation; but he overcame by the grace of the Lord. We realize how Satan frequently threatens and devours at the time of our weakness. This is truly one of his master tactics. His plot is to intimidate people. As a lion roars to cow and devour, Satan in like manner threatens believers so that they may be defeated through fear. How often all he does is merely threaten and nothing else. Those who are not intimidated recognize its vanity. Those who accept his threatening will encounter what is threatened. Are we not frequently faced with false alarms? Why should we be afraid of him?

(f) He causes pride: "Lest being puffed up he fall into the condemnation of the devil" (1 Tim. 3.6). Many Christians profess well in their spiritual life, and they are also fruitful in their service. Then, Satan seeks opportunity to work by causing them to be puffed up and fall. We have often witnessed great spiritual warriors and revivalists fall because of this sin. For this is the frequently-used device of Satan. He deceives man into counting the grace of God as his own. When grace begins to work in man's heart, Satan causes him to develop self-esteem, the man thinking that he now is different from ordinary people. He considers himself to be a

wonder. Satan wants man to be puffed up since this is the Tempter's own nature.

(g) He stirs people to do things beyond God's will: "Satan stood up against Israel, and moved David to number Israel" (1 Chron. 21.1). God had not commanded David to number the people of Israel. It was Satan who moved David to do this thing that was beyond God's will because he loves to have men suffer the wrath of God along with him. He will either hinder man from advancing, or push him too far. Today Christians are so careless as to deem all movings as being those of the Holy Spirit, not realizing that Satan can also move people. To number the children of Israel and of Judah cannot be counted as constituting a grievous sin, yet it was outside of God's will. So that Satan's instigation proved to be successful. Due to the lack of spiritual discernment, believers sometimes are moved to do a thing which, because it does not appear to be bad in itself, they judge themselves to have been moved to do by the Holy Spirit. Nevertheless, we should not look at things on the basis of their being good or bad in order to determine the source of inspiration. We should only decide by judging whether or not such things are the will of God. For outside of God's will there certainly do exist *many* good things!

(h) He beguiles people to disbelieve in God's word (Gen. 3.1). In Genesis 2.17 God had explicitly ordered man not to eat the fruit of the tree of good and evil; but the Devil suggested: "Hath God said?" The entire Bible is the word of God which is effective in attacking Satan. This is why the Tempter is so afraid of it that he beguiles people to doubt that the Bible is in-

deed the word of God. What is surprising is that the majority of people who doubt the Bible are so-called believers and not those who are total strangers to the Christian faith. The Devil first entices men to doubt God's word, then to believe in the Devil's word, thus causing men to fall into sin (see Gen. 3). Such work has not yet ended from the time of the garden of Eden even up to this present day.

(i) He oppresses people with sickness (Acts 10.38). How very many are the wiles of the Devil. If he cannot stir people into rebellion in their spirit, he will attack them in their body. He will oppress them with sickness so that they cannot enjoy the blessing of resurrection life. Due to discomfort in body, believers are able to be weakened in stedfastness and watchfulness in the spirit. We frequently see how workers who are active in the work of Christ easily fall into sickness. This is because the Devil wishes them ill so that they will cease to do the Lord's work.

3. His stratagem against those who are in God's hand: "Jehovah said unto Satan, Hast thou considered my servant Job? for there is none like him in the earth, a perfect and upright man, one that feareth God, and turneth away from evil" (Job 1.8).

(a) He shoots his fiery darts (Eph. 6.16). Satan cannot easily employ his strategy of either enticing surreptitiously or threatening openly those valiant Christian soldiers, for they are strong enough to war against him. So he throws fiery darts at them according to his murderous nature (John 8.44), expecting to inflict deadly wounds on them so that they may not recover. However, we have the way to destroy him, and this is in believing

in the faithfulness of God: "taking up the shield of faith, wherewith ye shall be able to quench all the fiery darts of the evil one" (Eph. 6.16) — meaning, using faith as a shield to quench the fiery darts and not as a clamp to pull out the darts after being wounded. We place faith between ourselves and the Devil just as a shield can separate us from an enemy in battle. If the enemy wants to hurt us he has to penetrate the shield, but should the shield be sturdy enough, the enemy's sword or spear cannot reach us. Likewise, then, in our battle with Satan, we take up our faith in God as a shield, so that when the fiery darts of Satan approach us, they are destroyed by this faith and thus cannot hurt us. Yet we who hold the shield need to be aware of the direction of the Devil's attack — whether front, back, left or right. Trust in God and be watchful. Satan will not be able to succeed in his strategy.

(b) He spreads his snares (1 Tim. 3.7). Believers press on towards the goal (Phil. 3.14), they do not travel in circles. Satan hates to see great progress made by believers, so he secretly lays snares along the way to cause them to fall. When a runner suddenly hits something, he easily falls and is hurt greatly. Hence Satan lays his crafty snares everywhere with the intention of causing believers to fall so far that they can never recover. The secret of regaining victory against the Enemy is found in Psalm 25.15: "Mine eyes are ever toward Jehovah; for he will pluck my feet out of the net." At first glance this verse seems to be worded rather strangely, for in running through the way that is densely laid with snares our eyes should be on the road in order to avoid these snares. Why, then, in the words of the psalmist, should

our eyes be turned upward towards the Lord in heaven? For if we face heaven and run forward, will we not fall to our death in these snares? We need to know here that the nets spread by the Devil may not be physical in nature and hence are not easy to detect. And even if we should know where they are, the result will be that we will so concentrate our attention on them and exert our uttermost strength to escape from them that we shall be unable to press on. For this reason we must look to God, for He knows where the nets are and *He* will pluck our feet from these nets. He will watch over our every step till we reach the goal.

(c) He practices his wiles (Eph. 6.11). If a person chooses Christ and abides in Him, the Devil has no wiles other than enticing him to depart from his position in Christ and to lead him away from Christ afterward. But we must follow the advice of Ephesians 6.13: "Take up the whole armor of God, that ye may be able to withstand in the evil day."

(d) He accuses believers (Rev. 12.10). Satan notices our every movement. He always seeks opportunity to accuse us that we may be judged along with him. But we should "overcome him because of the blood of the Lamb" (Rev. 12.11). For "the blood of Jesus his Son cleanseth us [continuing present tense] from all sin" (1 John 1.7). The blood of Jesus cleanses us today. His blood is our redemption price; it renders Satan's accusation ineffective. If perchance a believer sins, he will not feel condemned if he has asked for the cleansing of the precious blood of Christ. Otherwise, he will give ground to the Enemy.

(e) He corrupts our faith (2 Cor. 11.3). We ought

to have a simplicity and purity towards Christ such as a pure virgin has towards her husband. The Devil tries to defile us by seducing us to be unfaithful to Christ and fall into sin. We may overcome him by using the word in 1 John 2.14: "the word of God abideth in you, and ye have overcome the evil one." For God's word is the Sword of the Holy Spirit (Eph. 6.17). Satan will be wounded if we counterattack with the Sword of the Spirit. When the Lord Jesus was himself tempted, He used the word of the Scriptures to overcome Satan. Hence let the word of God dwell richly in our own hearts (Col. 3.16) that we may overcome the Evil One. As soon as we are tempted and attacked, we can instantly recall some appropriate Scripture which we fully believe. And thus we shall defeat our Foe. This is what using the word of God to overcome the Enemy means.

(f) He fashions himself as an angel of light (2 Cor. 11.14). If Satan should appear in his natural form, he would be recognized by watchful believers and thus be rejected. Hence he fashions himself as an angel of light in order to deceive believers into unconsciously walking a deceitful path. He pretends to be the voice of God and the guidance of the Holy Spirit so that believers who are zealous to do the will of God will hastily follow it. He also counterfeits truth to make people accept him. This scheme of his seems to be quite difficult for them to overcome. Yet the Scripture teaches us as follows: "prove the spirits . . . Ye are of God, my little children, and have overcome them: because greater is he that is in you than he that is in the world" (1 John 4.1,4). We can overcome false spirits by leaning on the Holy Spirit within us. And if we cannot decide whether the leading

is of God or not, we should first adopt a neutral attitude and pray: "O God, I will do whatever comes from You; but I will reject all that is of Satan. Please prove to me where this guidance comes from." God will no doubt make it clear. Constant practice brings in healthy spiritual life.

(g) He persecutes fiercely (Rev. 2.10). The wiles of the Devil are manifold. He will use all kinds of means to hinder the spiritual advance of the believer. When he finds he cannot block the advance, he will use persecution to put the believer in prison so that the latter is unable to work for the Lord anymore. He even expects this believer to fall. For this reason, all who love self and are mindful of themselves are no match for Satan; for as they are threatened with deadly persecution they shall lose the will to resist. But the faithful of the Lord have already put life and death out of their mind. Although they may encounter bonds and tribulations everywhere, even to the point of death, yet "they loved not their life even unto death" (Rev. 12.11). And thus shall they overcome Satan: "this is the victory that hath overcome the world, even our faith" (1 John 5.4). How, then, can any chains shake their hearts?

(h) He hinders answers to the prayers of the saints (Dan. 10.12–13). "Fear not, Daniel; for from the first day that thou didst set thy heart to understand, and to humble thyself before thy God, thy words were heard: and I am come for thy words' sake" (v.12). Even before Daniel's prayer was finished, the answer was already on the way. "But the prince of the kingdom of Persia withstood me one and twenty days" (v.13). This passage shows how Satan tries to block the answer to the prayer

of the saints. Was it too hard for Daniel to pray and fast for twenty-one days before he got the answer? Today Satan is still using this delaying tactic to answered prayer in order to make the believer's heart to faint. Let us overcome him by implementing into our lives the word in Luke 18.1: that we "ought always to pray, and not to faint." Let us hold on to our request, and if we do, we shall indeed overcome. Some may think if we pray in faith, then to pray once is sufficient. Though in certain instances this is true, it is also true in other instances that we need greater faith to pray without fainting. We should know that as we pray, the answer has already come from God's throne. Yet at that very moment there arises great conflict in the spiritual realm. We ought to persevere in prayer, asking God to "destroy the works of the devil." And thus shall our prayer hit the mark. We maintain an attitude of not quitting before we have the answer. Though the Foe attempts to hinder, heavenly angels will fight for us.

Four—How to Overcome the Tempter

"He that overcometh shall inherit these things" (Rev. 21.7).

1. We ought to know that it is not we who fight the Devil but it is God who does. The Devil is in the supernatural realm, whereas we dwell in the natural world. Our warfare is not against flesh and blood, but against the world-rulers of this darkness. So that for the ones who live in the natural world to fight against the spiritual forces in the supernatural realm, their defeat is certain. Hence, in our battle we *ask God* to fight for us by taking God's almighty power as our own power. In each conflict we *confess* this to be God's battle. All we do is to exercise our will to choose the victory of God over the gain of Satan. By attacking Satan with the supernatural almighty power of God, our victory over him is certain: "the God of peace shall bruise Satan under your feet shortly" (Rom. 16.20). Satan is under the feet of the Lord Jesus. Since we are united with the Lord, Satan is under *our* feet as well. It is not *we* who are able to bruise Satan under our feet; only the God of peace can put Satan there.

2. *Let us always put ourselves under the precious blood of Jesus lest we be condemned.* What the Devil fears most is the blood of Christ. Through the shedding of His blood Jesus breaks the head of the Devil (the real meaning of "bruise" in Genesis 3.15 is "break"). As the saints rely on the precious blood of the Lord and assume the attitude of Romans 6.11, Satan is defeated. "They [the brethren] overcame him [Satan] because of the blood of the Lamb" (Rev. 12.11). Our victory comes from the blood of Christ. The reason why believers are frequently attacked and accused by the Enemy is because they give ground to him through sinning. The basis of the Enemy's attack is sin. We thus need to assume the attitude that sin shall not have dominion over us. Even so, this will not prevent the Enemy from accusing and then attacking us, because we sometimes give ground unknowingly. Therefore, we must continuously put ourselves under the precious blood lest we be attacked. True, there may indeed be sin; nevertheless, the precious blood has already redeemed!

Thank the Lord, for the blood of Christ not only saves us but also gives us eternal victory in our Christian life.

3. We shall overcome if we are transformed by the word of God: "The word of God abideth in you, and ye have overcome the evil one" (1 John 2.14). The word of God is the word of the Scriptures. Having stored God's word in our heart, we will, in time of emergency, be reminded by the Holy Spirit of the word in one verse or several verses which can become our present refuge. It is as if we are hiding there, and in trusting the power of God's word we find the Enemy rendered powerless. The Scripture word which the Holy Spirit reminds us of increases our strength and courage, because every word of God is full of power: it is living and effective. We therefore ought to keep God's word fully in our heart—thus preventing Satan from any gain and defeating him completely.

4. Resist the Devil with our will. There is a will in us which is like our helm. If we use our will, saying to the Devil, "I do not permit you to enter into my heart, I will not give this right to you," then he will draw back from us. Do you acknowledge that *this* is the state and condition of *your* will? Otherwise, the reverse will be the result. We should obey God on the one hand and resist the Devil on the other. So shall the Enemy flee from us (see James 4.7). For example, if a peddler comes and you will not buy, he will naturally leave you after being resisted. But if you bargain with him for a lower price, you will soon buy this merchandise. Today many Christians lack the will of total resistance towards the Devil. And in thus bargaining with him, they fall into the trap of the Enemy. Resist the Devil with faith (1

Peter 5.8,9). In the power of God, say to Satan, "In the almighty name of the victorious Lord Jesus, I resist you." By assuming this attitude of faith and having resisted, we will find God causing Satan to flee according to His word. Praise God, Satan has fled, and you are more than conquerors through the Lord who loved us. When Satan came to tempt the Lord, our Lord gave no ground to him but immediately resisted and rebuked him (Matt. 16.23). We should be alert towards the Devil and firm in our word of resistance.

5. *Ask God and do not reason with the Devil:* "Michael the archangel, when contending with the devil ... said, The Lord rebuke thee" (Jude 9). Many believers do not ask God to rebuke Satan as soon as the latter moves; they instead listen to him and reason with his plot. In such a circumstance as that, they can hardly resist. It is important, therefore, that we ask God to rebuke Satan as soon as he begins speaking so as to prevent him from even finishing his speech. We believe God will immediately rebuke him, and he will trouble us no more. A certain believer once said, "According to my opinion, I will allow Satan to finish what he wants to say, and then I will know how to answer him." This is wrong! We must not answer the Devil; we must not let him converse with us. Otherwise, we shall be like Eve who listened to the word of Satan and even answered him, thus causing enormous distresses and evils to follow. Do not be afraid of losing friendship with Satan. Do not be afraid to be too hard on him. When he comes, ask the Lord to rebuke him. This assures us of our constant victory in the Lord.

6. *Do not give ground to the Enemy even in small*

things. We usually are careful in big things so that Satan cannot succeed in his devices: but in small things we tend to be careless, and hence we suffer defeats. Because of a thought or a word, we fall into the snares of the Devil. But if we can be faithful in small things, we will be faithful in big things. Always be watchful lest we "give place to the devil" (Eph. 4.27), but instead "give no occasion to the adversary" (1 Tim. 5.14); for without a factory the Devil is unable to manufacture any sin. If, though, we give place in our heart to the Enemy, and even though it be a tiny parcel of ground, the Devil will produce sin. We should never be negligent in the small matters of our lives. Let us realize that the Devil can, and will, penetrate the whole body through such small matters. But what are the occasions given to the Devil? These are (1) our unrighteousness, (2) our sin, and (3) our fear of him (that is to say, we do not have an active will to resist him, but are afraid of provoking his wrath by resisting). These grounds must be eliminated, or else the Enemy will never leave. I recall a story which can help to illustrate this matter. A certain traveler had set up a tent in the desert. A donkey asked the man for permission to thrust its head into the tent because it was cold outside. After a while, it asked to put its neck into the tent; later, it also asked to be allowed to place its two legs inside; and before long, its entire body was inside the tent! But now there was not room for both. And since the traveler could not drive the donkey away, he himself had to go outside the tent and allow the animal to stay in the tent! If believers today are complacent in small things, a little leaven will leaven the whole lump. The Devil will advance ten *feet* if he is given but one *inch*. Let us totally destroy his factory in us by the power of the Lord.

7. *Preserve a heart of love:* "to whom ye forgive anything, I forgive also ... that no advantage may be gained over us by Satan" (2 Cor. 2.10,11). An unloving and unforgiving heart usually gives place to the Devil. An unforgiving spirit opens the door to the works of Satan. If believers know more concerning the things in the spiritual realm, they will not be unloving and unforgiving. For should the adversities and persecutions which we suffer appear to come from men, we nonetheless discern the fact that behind every misunderstanding, every cutting word or every distress lie the evil spirits. Our warfare is not against flesh and blood, but against the evil spirits. Whatever happens, we need to ask the Lord to rebuke Satan and destroy his work. Loving and forgiving enable us to be more than conquerors.

8. *Be especially careful of our speech:* "let your speech be, Yea, yea; Nay, nay: and whatsoever is more than these is of the evil one" (Matt. 5.37). The Devil does not like Yea, yea and Nay, nay; he loves yea as nay and nay as yea. I once heard a zealous believer say, "It seems that I cannot control my mind. Sometimes I unconsciously take yea as nay, and nay as yea. Though I will to overcome this, I just cannot." Before anyone ever believed in the Lord his mind had been blinded by the Devil (2 Cor. 4.4). But then after he is saved the Holy Spirit enters into his spirit and enlightens him so that gradually all the coverings in his mind are being removed (for no one can understand all the truth immediately after believing). By consecration and obedience to the Holy Spirit his mind is being renewed (see Rom.

12.2). Having put off the old man, the spirit of his mind is renewed (Eph. 4.22–23). Then he is able to say what he wants to say, which is, to say Yea, yea and Nay, nay. Though believers may have a beautiful life, their mind may still be disturbed by unclean and disobedient thoughts. This is because the evil spirits send these evil thoughts into the believer's mind and try to lodge there. Sometimes they may dull the mind and paralyze it so that the believer will confuse yea and nay. Such spiritual disease can be overcome through prayer and the help of the Holy Spirit. Remember that "if any stumbleth not in word, the same is a perfect man" (James 3.2).

9. *Be watchful in dealing with others:* "looking to thyself, lest thou also be tempted" (Gal. 6.1). It is comparatively easier to restore a person to righteousness than to restore him from perverse thoughts, words or deeds. Oftentimes in helping others the believer himself may be tempted. Hence a worker needs to be always on the alert to discover the wiles of Satan. There is no day we can say we are completely out of danger.

10. *Always acknowledge that the Enemy is under our control:* "Behold, I have given you authority ... over all the power of the enemy: and nothing shall in any wise hurt you" (Luke 10.19). What the Enemy has is "power"; but what we have is "authority." In spite of the fact that our personal "power" is not as great as his, the "authority" we receive from the Lord causes him to be subject to us. We have no need to struggle over power; all we need to do is to command with "authority." Surprising as it may seem, "power" is no match for "authority." Therefore, let us first obtain this authority through union with Christ's death, and then

moment by moment let us use this authority by faith to overcome and to subdue all the powers of darkness. Thus shall we have victory over whatever circumstances come our way.

Five—The Limit Placed upon the Tempter

1. *Without God's permission, no temptation can come upon the believer:* "Jehovah said unto Satan, Behold, all that he hath is in thy power; *only* . . ." (Job 1.12); "Simon, Simon, behold, Satan *asked* to have you . . ." (Luke 22.31). Each time we are tempted, we should remember that all temptations are with the Father's permission. Behind any temptation there is the hand of God allowing it. Let us maintain this attitude of faith that Satan cannot do anything against us without God our Father's permission. He cannot secretly add any more to it.

2. *The reason why God permits Satan to tempt us.* Without temptation we would become self-reliant. Before Peter was "sifted as wheat" by the Devil (Luke 22.31), he was most self-reliant. But after being sifted, he knew how undependable was his own strength. He then received the power from on High to perform tremendous work. If, for example, a little child is unwilling to follow his father and chooses to go his own way, he will hurry back to his father for protection when he encounters a snake. Likewise, without temptation a saint in his early stage of spiritual life will tend to drift away from the heavenly Father. But as we sense in the spiritual realm the presence of the evil spirits who

try to tempt and hurt us at every turn, we will trust in God and dare not be self-reliant: "There was given to me . . . a messenger of Satan to buffet me," said Paul, "that I should not be exalted overmuch" (2 Cor. 12.7). In our flesh there is no good, but how many will consciously acknowledge this? Because of this, God permits the Enemy to tempt us. Sometimes He even lets us fail so that we may know ourselves and cease from being self-reliant. This was the experience of Job. Furthermore, without being tempted we will not voluntarily appropriate the victory of Calvary. Because of temptation, there is the chance of victory—the necessity as well as the possibility of apprehending the victory of Calvary. Since we know the true meaning of temptation which is something unavoidable, we should ask God to give us the victory in Christ. We may know why God allows us to be tempted by reading 1 Corinthians 5.5 and Job 2.3. (To be tempted is *not* sin, but yielding to temptation *is*—see Heb. 4.16.)

3. The confinement of temptation: "There hath no temptation taken you but such as man can bear ["but such as is common to man"—KJV]: but God is faithful, who will not suffer you to be tempted above that ye are able; but will with the temptation make also the way of escape, that ye may be able to endure it" (1 Cor. 10.13). There are seven points in this verse that we should know:

(a) Temptation is common to all. Someone may think that his environment and position is so unique that no one else has it, and therefore the temptation he suffers is special. He should know that temptation is common to all: "but such as is common to man."

(b) Remember: "God is faithful." We can only fail if God fails. But He is faithful. So we must trust and not fail.

(c) All temptations are endurable: "such as man can bear." The temptation permitted by God will not be overwhelming, and hence, at the beginning of temptation we must not adopt a passive attitude and let the Devil do what he wishes.

(d) There is a "way of escape" to every temptation. Hence there is victory each time.

(e) God will "make also the way of escape" when there seems to be no way.

(f) Sometimes endurance is the way out: "can bear."

(g) To be tempted is no sin, but yielding to temptation is: "that ye may be able to endure it."

4. *The all-powerful preservation of God:* "we know that whosoever is begotten of God sinneth not; but he that was begotten of God keepeth himself, and the evil one toucheth him not" (1 John 5.18); "the Lord is faithful, who shall establish you, and guard you from the evil one" (2 Thess. 3.3). Be strong in the Lord and trust in His protection. Commit all your spirit and soul and body to the Lord, and trust in Him, for He will do it. Believe and act in faith as though you are already being kept. Such act of faith will secure the keeping of God.

5. *Pray:* "Our Father . . ., deliver us from the evil one" (Matt. 6.9,13). As we pray, let us not merely remember ourselves and God. We should not forget Satan, "the evil one," either. We must ask God to deliver us from the wiles, deceit, control, influence, attack and snare of that Evil One. We shall be delivered if we so

pray. But how is it that we can be delivered from the Evil One? The answer is to be found in these words: "for thine [God's] is [1] the kingdom, [2] and the power, [3] and the glory, for ever. Amen" (Matt. 6.13 mg.). These do not belong to Satan. They are God's "for ever. Amen." This prayer of deliverance is based on God's kingdom, power and glory; and therefore, it cannot go unanswered; for if God does not deliver us from the Evil One, His kingdom and power and glory shall suffer. Since kingdom, power and glory do not belong to the Enemy, why then should we endure his attack, oppression and ravage?

6. *The intercessory prayer of the heavenly High Priest:* "I pray not that thou shouldest take them from the world, but that thou shouldest keep them from the evil one" (John 17.15). What have we to fear since we now have our Great High Priest praying for us? We ought always to trust in the intercession of the Lord Jesus that it is most *effective,* believing that God the Father will secretly keep us from the Evil One because of the prayer of Christ. Do not allow the Enemy to suggest to us that we shall soon meet danger. Instead, we should have confidence in the intercessory prayer of our Great High Priest, believing confidently that God the Father will surely keep us from the ravaging of the Evil One.

7. *The end of the Enemy.* Satan the Adversary shall be cast out of heaven to the earth (Rev. 12.7–9). He shall be bound with chains and thrown into the abyss (Rev. 20.1–3). After the thousand years of the reign of Christ, he will be set free temporarily, and he will deceive the nations which are in the four corners of the earth so

as to stage a counterattack against God. In the end, however, he shall be cast into the lake of fire (Rev. 20.7–10). Since the Enemy is destined to fail, why should we not rise up and advance? Should we not be even more courageous by our knowing that the defeat of the Enemy is predestined?

We should always stand on Romans 6.11. Reckon ourselves to be dead to sin but alive to God. Take up the whole armor of God so as to overcome the world, the lusts of the flesh, and the Devil. Be the elite soldiers of God and fight the good fight. Cast down the strongholds of Satan and bring every thought into captivity to the obedience of Christ (2 Cor. 10. 4–5). Let us not only be kept whole, but let us even be able to challenge the Tempter by our being strong prayer-warriors. Frustrate the devices of the evil spirits and walk and work together with Christ. Triumph today and reign in the age to come. Amen.

TITLES YOU
WILL WANT TO HAVE

By Watchman Nee

By Stephen Kaung

ORDER FROM:

Christian Fellowship Publishers, Inc.
11515 Allecingie Parkway
Richmond, Virginia 23235